O9-BHK-547

SIMPLIFIED CAKE DECORATING

ILLUSTRATED

REVISED BY
ELIZABETH DE UNDA
AND
EDITH LATIMER

FOURTEENTH EDITION

Published by
AUGUST THOMSEN & CO., INC.
37-28 56th STREET, WOODSIDE, NEW YORK 11377

August Thomsen & Company, Inc.
37-28 56th Street, Woodside, New York 11377

PRINTED IN THE UNITED STATES OF AMERICA

"About the Authors"

Elizabeth de Unda, Food Editor for a New York Society magazine, and Edith Latimer, Home Economist and Radio Lecturer, are the owners and operators of the famous "Buffet Party Catering Service and Catering School."

Their canapes and hors d'oeuvre were voted THE BEST BY THE PRESS at an invitation showing at the Waldorf Astoria Hotel. They are the only caterers to have served the "World Series" year after year. They have made and decorated President Eisenhower's birthday cake for his Republican Club parties. They also have made numerous decorated cakes for Katharine Cornell, Arthur Godfrey and many other prominent celebrities.

Because of their thorough step-by-step method taught with all "Ateco" tubes and appliances, only a few lessons are required to master the fundamentals of this interesting art.

PREFACE

Interest in food decorating is increasing rapidly in today's society. Food prepared for special occasions, when decorated, adds so much of your personal touch to the affair, as well as make your guests feel that you were thinking of them in preparing for the specific occasion.

This book has been prepared with thought and care to enable the student and housewife to learn the art of cake decorating—with a tube for every purpose.

The ability to know what can be made with the decorating tubes and how to use them is the basis of your decorating knowledge. In this edition we will endeavor to acquaint you with the tubes, with instructions as to their various uses, as well as detailed directions for making icing flowers. We have also included throughout the book many illustrations of cakes for the more popular occasions during the year. However, please do not be limited to the decorations and designs shown in this book. They are only ideas and suggestions. Your own originality and particular adaptations of decorations will make your food truly original and truly artistic.

Today everyone wishes to express himself in some artistic way, and it is almost limitless what may be accomplished by availing oneself of the use of these diversified tubes. As you decorate your birthday or party cakes, many ideas will present themselves to you that will be your very own, individual and original.

AUGUST THOMSEN & CO., INC.

DECORATING TUBES

On page 8 you will see a complete assortment of Decorating Tubes numbered from 1 to 105. From this group you may select those tubes you find most interesting for the various flowers you wish to make. There is a very minute difference in some of this selection; however, each tube has its definite individual purpose. These tubes are easy to work with and they may be used with a canvas bag, plastic bag, neoprene rubber bag, vegetable parchment paper made in the form of a cone, or a decorating syringe.

After making your cone of paper, cut off the tip, drop in the tube, allowing it to extend about one half inch. (This paper cone is only applicable to Butter Cream Icing. Recipe on page 51.) It is most important—at all times—to push the Butter Cream down in the forward part of your cone allowing the flowers or designs to flow out easily.

The plastic, or the neoprene rubber bags may be used the same way as the paper cones explained above, or the tips of these bags may be cut so that the coupling fits into them. The canvas decorating bag must be used in conjunction with the coupling. With the coupling you may use different tubes without emptying the icing, simply unscrew the coupling nut, remove tube and replace with the next tube desired. These bags are to be used with the conventional Royal Icing (recipe on page 51) or any of the other decorating icings.

Standard Ornamenting Tube

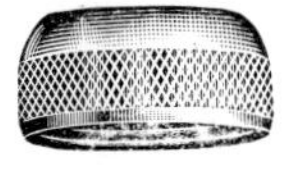

Coupling Nut

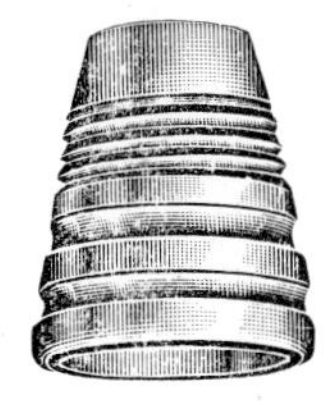

Coupling

We illustrate a few of the various flowers, designs, and borders on the following pages. The numbers on the left indicate the number of the tube used. On the page following each illustration you will find an explanation of each tube, and instruction for its use in detail.

On the following pages we explain how each and every design made with the entire line of 100 tubes is accomplished.

Set No. 785—100 tubes of the above designs in box with individual compartment for each tube.

PLAIN TUBES

No. 1. This tube is used to make lines, fine stems, scrolls, vines, stamens on large flowers, and the little yellow "stick up" stamens in the lilies of the valley. It is most adaptable for fine writing on cake, which may later be decorated with the phantasy flowers for beauty.

No. 2. Tube is used for a great number of purposes in decorating, many of which we list for you here, i.e. small lettering and writing, making the green balls which form the center of the wild rose, the apple blossom, the poinsettia.

No. 3. This one is for use in making thicker scrolls, putting finishing dots in phantasy flowers on cup cakes, and for the tiny buds for the lilies of the valley and lilac sprays.

No. 4. With this tube, as indicated in the picture, we show the progressive stages of the making of a dove. Pipe the body and without withdrawing tube pipe the head, which is made by moving the tube slightly upwards. Pipe the left wing onto the dove, then the right wing, which must be smaller so that about half of the left wing shows above the right. On illustration of the completed dove, the most prominent wing is the left one (although it does not appear so). The right must be smaller or else the left wing will be hidden from view. No. 1 tube is used for making the eye and beak by placing a dot in the right place. This we find to be an extremely popular motif, especially on an all white cake.

No. 5. Shows a rabbit in progressive stages. Start by using tube No. 2 and pipe the left hind leg, as shown in picture. Now with a No. 5 tube make upper part of leg a little wider, rounding it out nicely. Continue with body, controlling the pressure so that there is a slight swell in the center. We show a separate illustration of the head on the right side of the plate. This should be piped right after the body, without withdrawing the tube. Taper the head gracefully by drawing tube away slowly. Now take tube No. 2 and pipe the right hind leg, working it nicely out of the hindquarters. With the same tube make the front legs, tail, and a small dot for the eye.

No. 6. Is used primarily for classic work. To make the attractive side border, do not hold tube upright, but rather at an angle. Start with a small bead, gradually increasing size until center is reached, then decrease the size of the beads in symmetry with the first side. Do not draw tube away until each section is finished, as this would break the continuity of the motif.

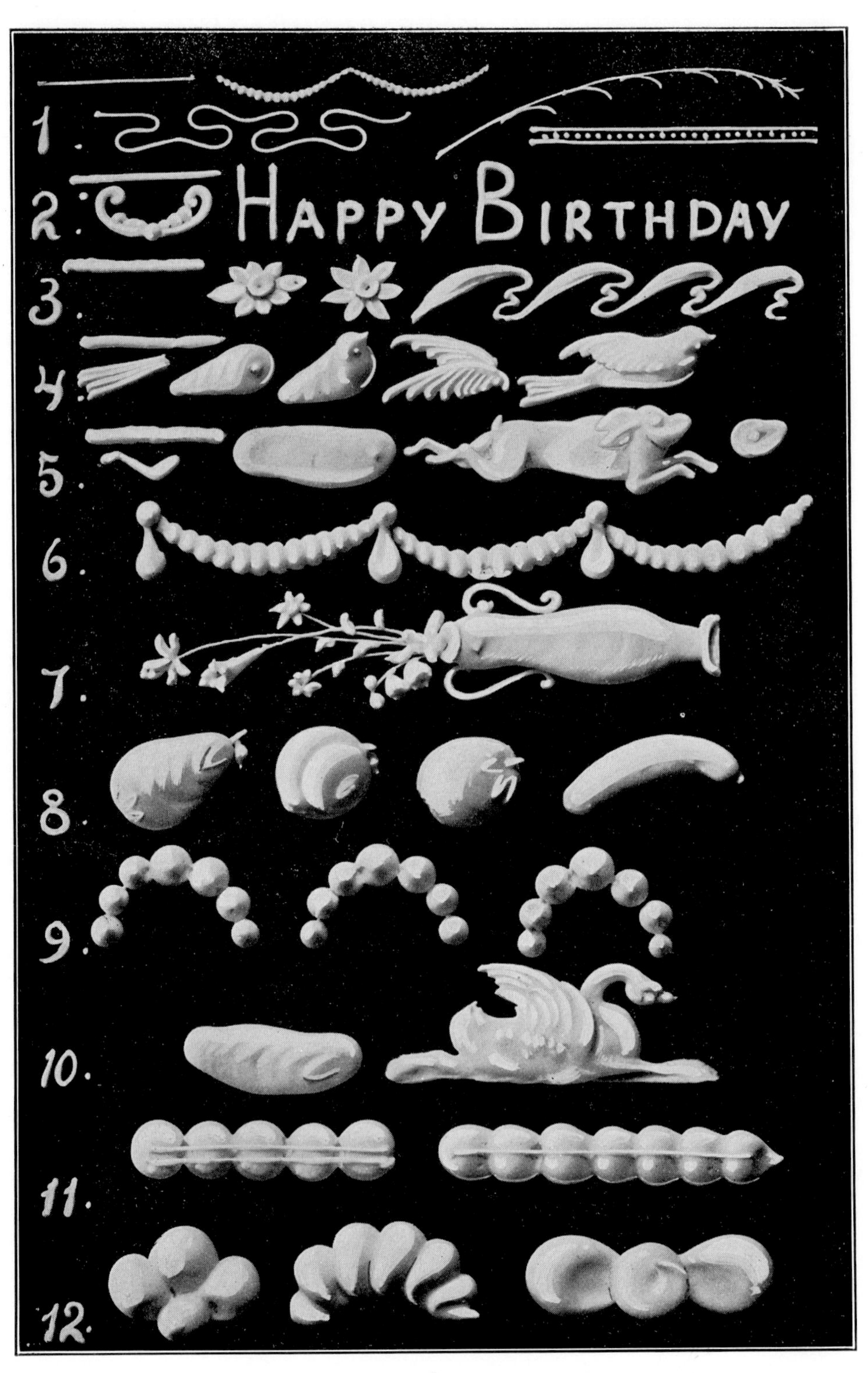

Number indicates tube used to make design.

No. 7. The vase in the picture is made with tube No. 7. The base and handles are made with tube No. 2, and the stems of the small flowers are made with tube No. 1. Overpipe several times to get the best effect on the handles and base.

No. 8. Many decorators use No. 8 for making loops on the side of the cake, using No. 2 tube for dot at the top of each loop. We suggest that you use a contrasting color for an interesting effect. This tube is also used to make a large assortment of fruit, i.e. pears, apples, peaches, bananas. No. 2 tube is to be used for the stems.

No. 9. This tube may be used instead of No. 8 if you desire your decoration to be of a larger size.

No. 10. The body of the swan illustrated in No. 10 is easy to make. Use tube No. 10 to pipe the body. Change to tube No. 3 and pipe out the neck and head, allowing these to flow out of the body, thus giving the swan a natural appearance. Pipe on the left wing first; make the right one smaller so that the left one is not hidden from view. The swan is finished by piping on the tail, using a few curved, upward strokes. A few choppy strokes around the swan will give the appearance of gliding on water.

No. 11. There are a number of borders made with this tube, two of which are shown in the illustration. The first border is made holding the tube in an upright position, bearing in mind that beads are made very close together. For the second border the tube should be held at an angle. Remember, do not withdraw tube until entire border is finished. The thread line across the beads is made with tube No. 1. We have found that these two illustrated borders are excellent to use at the base of a small cake which has been placed on an iced disk.

No. 12. This is suggested as an exceptionally good tube for the making of petits-fours, French pastry, macaroons, and tea cakes, and for decorating squares and diamond shaped small iced cakes.

If you have faithfully followed and practiced your decorating, you will enjoy making the lovely Swan Cake pictured on opposite page.

Inasmuch as a Swan Cake should be pure white—both in batter and icing, you will find an excellent recipe for each below.

WHITE CAKE RECIPE (FOR SWAN)

1 cup sugar
½ cup butter
½ cup milk

1½ cups cake flour
2 teaspoons baking powder
¼ teaspoon salt
3 egg whites

Beat egg whites until stiff, add ½ cup of the sugar. Set this aside. Cream the butter and remaining sugar gradually, while constantly beating. Combine and sift flour, baking powder and salt; and add, alternating with milk. Fold in egg whites. Now add one teaspoon of vanilla. Bake in a moderate oven (350°F.) for 45 minutes. This may be baked in a round 9″ pan. When cool cut through the center and spread with filling.

WATER LILY ICING

2 cups granulated sugar
⅔ cup water

¼ teaspoon cream of tartar
2 egg whites—beaten stiff

Dissolve sugar, water and cream of tartar, and bring to the boiling point. Add 3 tablespoons of this syrup to beaten egg whites, beating constantly after adding each spoonful. Boil remaining syrup to 240°F. or until it spins a thread. Do not stir! Pour slowly over egg whites, beating constantly, until thick enough to stand up in peaks. Flavor with one teaspoon almond, or lemon extract. Spread quickly on cake, before the frosting becomes too stiff. This allows enough filling for a 9-inch, two layer cake, and frosting for the top and sides. After frosting the cake put on the swan and accompanying decorations.

THE SWAN CAKE

This cake was piped with the tubes shown on page 10 and is a splendid example of what can be done with plain tubes only. See page 12 for batter recipe and icing recipe.

Number indicates tube used to make design.

OPEN STAR TUBES

These decorating tubes offer a varied selection of designs, including stars, scrolls, writing tubes, border designs, floral sprays, wavy frolics for decorating the sides of the cake, the body and accompanying scrolls of the pineapple, individual rosettes, curved pipings, etc.; and are numbered 13 through 22 inclusive.

The star tubes are excellent for the beginner, who has not yet learned to make the true flowers so necessary for finished cake decoration.

No. 13. Is especially adapted to making pipings, straight and curved lines, scrolls, etc.

No. 14. This tube may be used as a dainty phantasy flower, and is very lovely on small cup cakes when used in a motif of pastel colors as shown here.

No. 15. Is an unusually good border tube. Start the border by using light pressures and moving up and down to get the fancy effect. Enlarge the design gradually by increasing the pressure very slowly. This enlarges the crinkled part of the border. When you draw the tube away, you will find this makes a curved line.

No. 16. Which is a six point star tube will enable you to make a pineapple. The pineapple leaves are made with the smallest leaf tube No. 65. Start making these leaves at the top of the pineapple, by using slight pressure and drawing up the tube about one half inch.
The base of the pineapple is made by running tube back and forth at least two times.

No. 17. By using a wavy motion of the tube one can obtain a crinkled effect. Diminish the pressure so that it tapers to a curved line at the finish. Now, make a scroll with the No. 3 tube, as shown in the picture on page 14. You may overpipe this hooked scroll a number of times to prevent too flat an effect. Space these designs evenly, and put finishing touches of beads in each center, as shown in picture.

No. 18. This is an extremely popular tube as it lends itself to easily moving the hand up and down, making each interesting and quite simple design.

Grouping 19–20–21. These tubes graduate in size. The variety of designs which can be obtained by their use is great, thus giving the decorator flexibility in both size and type. They are for making 8-point stars and interesting motifs on the side of the cake. With a little imagination such ideas as placing a contrasting colored dot in the center of the star for beauty and the artistic touch can be carried out.

With the large star tube you can control the size and thickness of the star by the pressure of your hand on the bag. Press the bag, release pressure, then lift the bag away from the surface. This will produce a thick star with a rounded top.

If you are a new student, practice making the star until you acquire perfection. This you will enjoy doing. There is no branch of the culinary art that gives more pleasure, and later on, the monetary returns available to one who has a working knowledge of each tube are exceptional.

Remember, as you acquire the basic "know-how" of decorating, and the use of these tubes, you will originate many unusual motifs.

It will amaze you how easily you may create the lovely—the beautiful!!

No. 22. This 9 pointed tube is used for making macaroons, tea cakes, whipped cream or meringue and potato borders or beveled effect. This tube makes a very wide scroll.

We suggest that you use a plastic bag which will hold a larger quantity than the paper cone, and which lends itself more satisfactorily to holding the batter.

On page 19 we are illustrating two interesting star cakes, one of which has at the center the space for writing such greetings as "Happy Birthday," "Happy Anniversary," etc. The second cake has the easy-to-make filled in star. This is done by pull up phantasy stars, using first the deep purple, highlighted by the smaller stars made with a lovely shade of lavender. Directions for mixing these colors are explained on page 52.

At a Sweet Sixteen birthday party,
a heart cake with roses and lilies of the valley
seems so original.

For Mother's Day, a bouquet of mixed flowers
is very appropriate.

This anniversary cake with the flowers
flowing down on to the cardboard base, which has been frosted,
is a very original idea.

Here's another anniversary cake.
The garland of flowers on one side
allows plenty of room for your message.

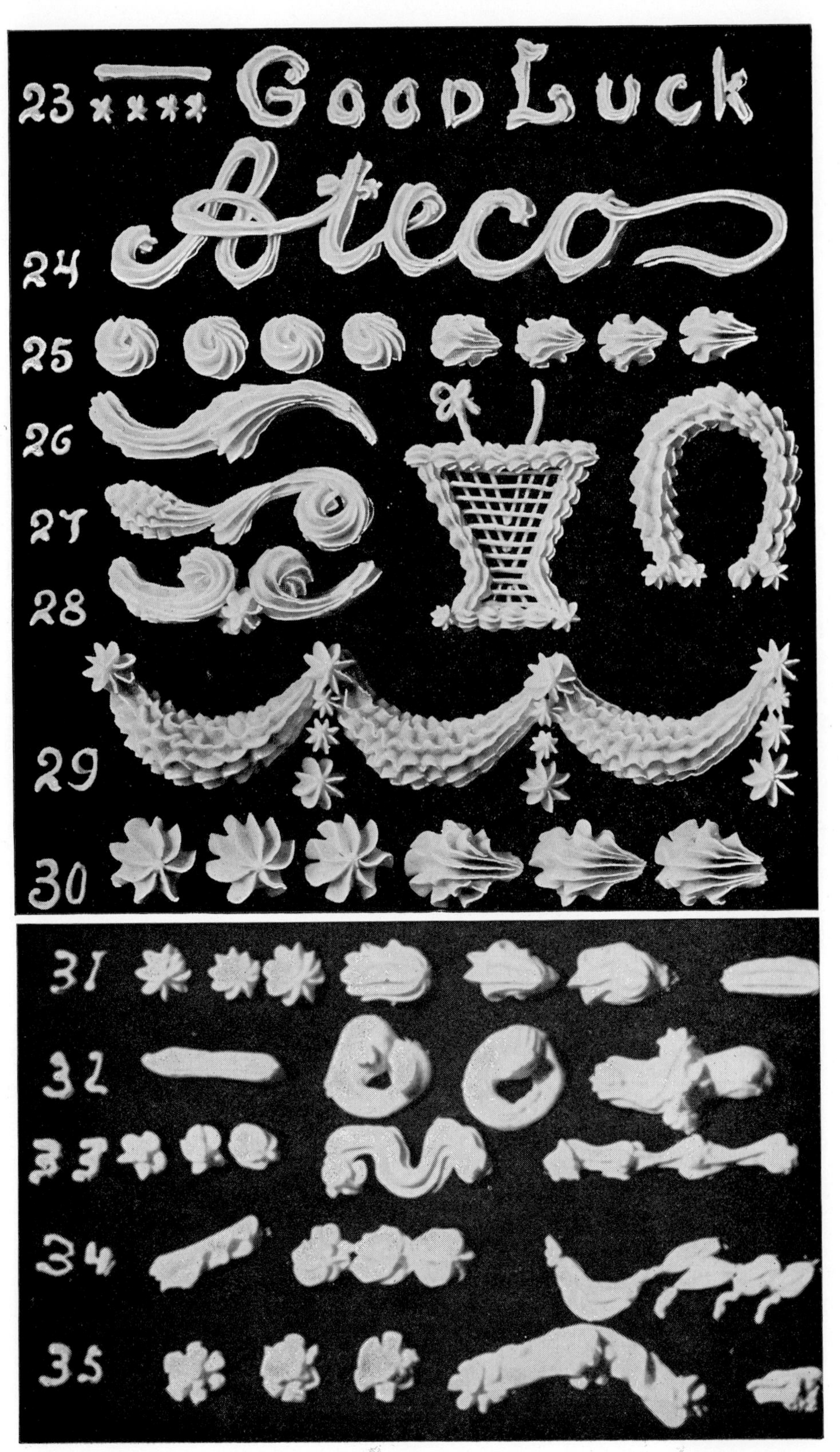
23
Good Luck
24
Ateco
25
26
27
28
29
30
31
32
33
34
35

CLOSED STAR TUBES

The dozen star tubes run from Nos. 23 to 35 inclusive. The variety of stars, shells and writing or lettering that may be made from these tubes is surprising. The variations in size and style offer the decorator an interesting and diversified choice and a chance to expand her originality.

Nos. 23 and 24 are five point stars.

Nos. 25 and 26 are six point stars.

No. 27 is a seven point star.

Nos. 28, 29 and 30 are eight point stars.

All stars must be evenly made so that both sides will correspond in size. To make the points outstanding, exert greater pressure before removing cone. Often during your practice work inspect the points of the star tubes, keeping them evenly spaced to insure a well-formed star.

Nos. 31, 32, 33, 34 and 35 are larger star tubes that lend themselves to the making of important looking borders. No. 32 is especially good for decorating deviled eggs. It also can be used for stuffing celery. For this type of decorating we suggest you use the large plastic bag.

One pretty design for the eggs is piling one rosette on top of the other. Of course the consistency of the egg yolk may be made to pass easily through any large star tube. Thick stars are made by always releasing the pressure of the hand on the bag before lifting.

Hold the bag vertically to the surface, a fraction of an inch above same.

By using stars of different sizes and pastel colors, a lovely border or beveled effect can be made. If you desire a pin wheel effect, while pushing the bag, turn slightly to the right. Place the cake on an attractive paper doily which extends a few inches from the base.

No. 28 makes a design very appropriate for the side of the cake. First pipe the design (as shown on opposite page), then overpipe once, completing the motif. Bear in mind that for a graceful finish, you must diminish the flow of cream at the end. Join these two motifs by placing a star between them.

BASKETS

Baskets are all made of similar design, and usually have flowers on, or coming out of them. By using tube No. 27 you may make a simple basket, as the more intricate ones will follow later. This, however, gives a basic design. A basket is generally outlined with some ornamental border.

The lattice work of this basket (illustrated on page 20) is made with tube No. 2. The outlining border is made with No. 27 tube.

A horseshoe is often used on a cake as a "good luck" omen for the opening of a new business. A very interesting cake is made by making a large horseshoe in the center of the cake. See illustration on page 23. This may be complemented by baby horseshoes spaced evenly around the sides of the cake.

HORSESHOE CAKE

- 1½ cups shortening
- 3½ cups brown sugar (packed)
- 5 cups cake flour
- 3 teaspoons soda
- 1 teaspoon salt
- 2 whole eggs
- 6 egg yolks
- 6 1 oz. squares unsweetened chocolate (melted)
- 3½ teaspoons vanilla
- 3 cups milk

Start oven 12 minutes before putting cake in oven at 350°. (Remember a dark cake is always baked at lower temperatures than a light cake). Grease and flour 2 12″ pans. Cream shortening and sugar well. Sift flour—measure—and resift with soda and salt three times. To creamed shortening and sugar add eggs and yolks—beating at low speed. Stir in chocolate and vanilla—add flour and milk alternately, beating until well blended—never beat too much after flour is added. Pour in prepared pans—bake at 350° for approximately 35 to 40 minutes, or until cake is done.

BUTTER CREAM ICING

This may be used for the filling and frosting of the cake. The same may be used to make the decorative horseshoes.

To three cups of creamed butter gradually add six cups of sifted confectioners' 4X or 10X sugar. Rum flavoring added to the above makes a delicious filling and icing.

GOOD LUCK

BIRTHDAYS

It is always gratifying to feel that there are those who are happy because we were born. A birthday party is a gathering of intimate and close friends which should always be celebrated with a decorated cake—whether large or small. There should be space for candles but not necessarily in "tell-tale" number. Use your favorite cake recipe or any one which you will find among the pages of our book. This is the type of cake where many different tubes may be introduced. You will need four or five types of phantasy flowers from tubes Nos. 13 to 19. These will accompany any of the various flowers, instructions for which you will find in later chapters. A simple birthday cake, however, may be made using all phantasy flowers in various sizes and pastel colors. Use tube No. 23 for inscribing your birthday greetings.

Many times you will wish to make the flowers appropriate for the month.

January	Carnation	July	Waterlily
February	Violet	August	Poppy
March	Daffodil	September	Aster or Morning Glory
April	Sweetpea or Daisy	October	Cosmos
May	Lily of the Valley	November	Chrysanthemum
June	Rose	December	Holly

It is also nice to know the "Birthstone of the month," which we are happy to include.

January	Garnet	July	Ruby
February	Amethyst	August	Sardonyx
March	Aquamarine	September	Sapphire
April	Diamond	October	Opal
May	Emerald	November	Topaz
June	Pearl	December	Turquoise

Do not think for a moment that these wonderful decorating tubes are limited to the decoration of cakes and canapés. You will find your molded creations more beautiful and interesting if you will use tube No. 31 for making large rosettes of avocado surrounding your mousse of aspic. This calls for a little cream cheese mixed with finely mashed avocado sprinkled with lemon juice. Be sure mixture is smooth—cheese is soft and avocado has no lumps or it will clog tube. Use tube No. 31 and your plastic bag—and may we add—your imagination. You will find the rich green combined with the delicate pastel shades of veal or chicken aspic will make your dish look like a regal production.

QUICK TOMATO ASPIC

- 1 envelope unflavored gelatin
- ½ cup cold tomato juice
- 1½ cups hot tomato juice
- ½ teaspoon salt
- ⅛ teaspoon pepper
- 1½ tablespoons lemon juice

Dissolve gelatine in cold tomato juice, then add hot juice, stir thoroughly. Add salt, pepper, and lemon juice and pour into a mold. Since this delicious aspic is solid red in color, you will find the addition of the above avocado decoration very beautiful.

MOLDED CRANBERRY, WALNUT SALAD

- 2 envelopes lemon flavored gelatin
- 2 cups cranberry sauce (quite thick)
- 3 cups hot water
- 1¼ cups crushed pineapple with juice
- ¾ cup chopped walnuts
- whipped cream
- mayonnaise

Dissolve gelatin in hot water. After straining cranberries (or putting through sieve) combine with pineapple and juice and walnuts and add to gelatin mixture. Chill until this is set, then unmold. Before serving decorate with mayonnaise which has been mixed with whipped cream. This can be used with any tube from Nos. 31 to 35 on any of your molded creations.

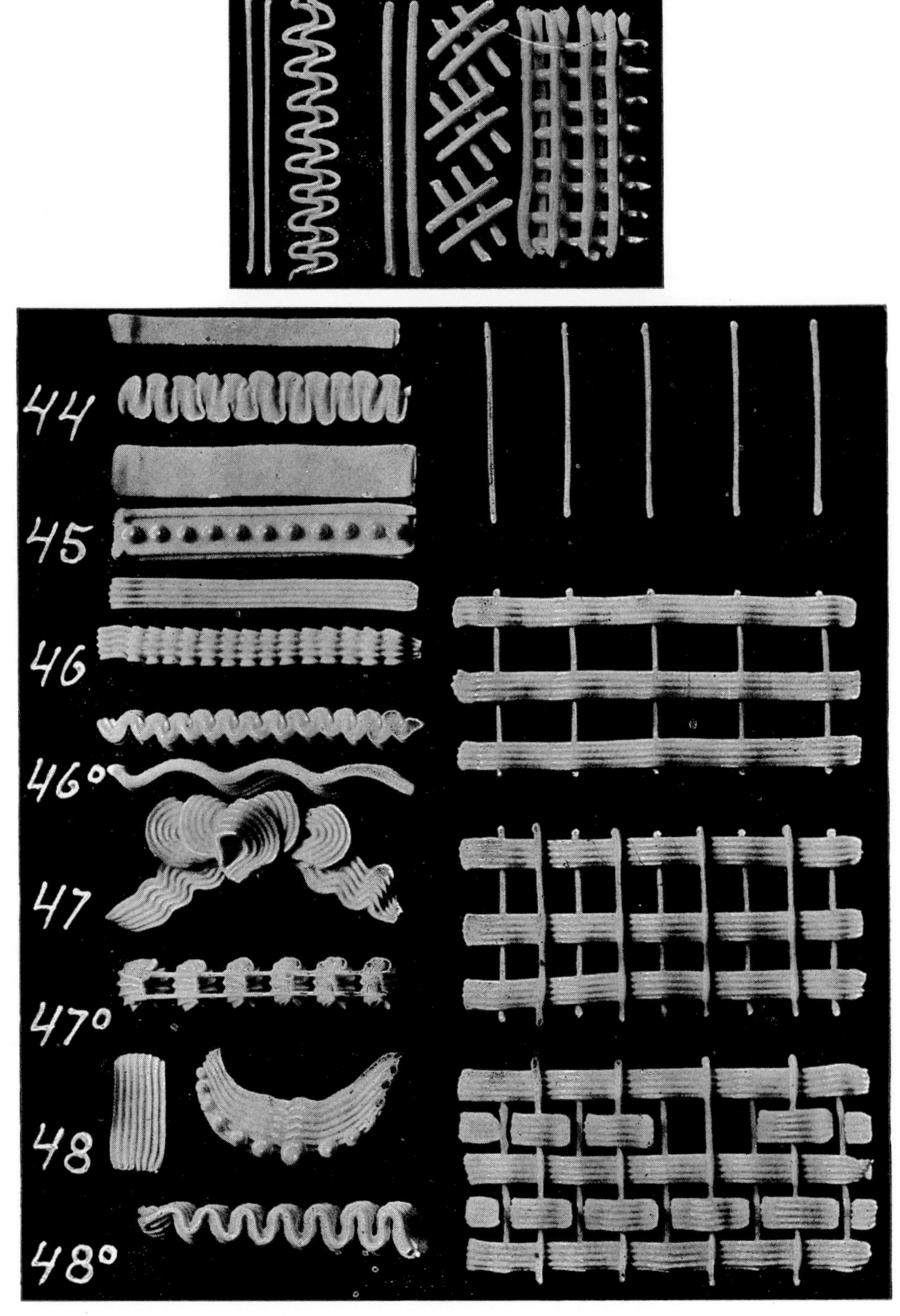

Number indicates tube used to make design.

DOUBLE LINE TUBES

Double line tubes are used when accurate spacing and double lines are required. The tubes come in Nos. 41, 42 and 43 which are small, medium and large respectively and are especially fine in finishing baskets and making scroll work.

PLAIN AND FANCY RIBBON TUBES

By following the illustrations on the opposite page you will see that the plain and fancy ribbon tubes run from Nos. 44 to 48°.

No. 44 is a flat tube created for making bows at the bottoms of simulated bouquets or for borders which are made by holding tube flat and moving from side to side with a wavy motion.

No. 45 is also a utility tube but is larger than No. 44. Your motifs may be made in any pastel color—overpiped with a fine white line, using No. 1 tube. You will doubtless find innumerable uses for this tube. Each aspiring decorator is interested in working out new designs. The illustrated designs on opposite page will suggest to you more attractive motifs.

No. 46 has serrations on one side and tube No. 46° has serrations on both sides. You may make the flat fancy ribbon (with the serrations on one side) and the closely crinkled ribbon, which is made with an up and down movement of the hand.

If you wish your border to be a little wider, use tube No. 47 as this tube is an eighth of an inch larger in size than tube No. 46.

No. 48° is the largest serrated tube and is often used for making bow knots which appear to tie together a bouquet of flowers for top cake decoration, or for fancy ribbons and for the wicker and crosslines on basket work. In a later chapter the basket work will be given in progressive steps with complete instructions.

GENERAL PLANNING OF CAKE DECORATING

You are at the stage where, before going on with the making of more elaborate flowers and various decorations, we believe we should emphasize the necessity of a thorough knowledge of cake making, and here are some tips involved in making frostings and icings.

First of all, consider the occasion and type of decorating you desire for your cake.

It is permissible to line the bottom of the cake pan with paper. If, during baking, you find that the cake is becoming too brown, place a piece of brown paper on top of the cake. Allow cakes to remain in their pans for about eight minutes after removing them from the oven. Then place upside down on cake racks to cool evenly.

When baking a white cake, a higher degree of heat is used—use a cooler oven for devil's food or gingerbread. Cupcakes baked in paper cups sometimes become too brown on the bottom. To prevent this place a pan turned upside down under cupcake pans. In making cakes using nuts or fruits, lightly dust with flour before adding them to the batter, thus preventing them from slipping to the bottom during baking.

It is imperative that all ingredients be measured carefully, as a perfect cake is light and even textured and the surface is slightly moist. Too much baking powder, sugar or shortening may make the cake fall, and too small an amount of liquid will make the cake uneven. Too much flour will cause the cake to be uneven or dry. Do not overbeat the batter as this tends to make the cake heavy.

Bake at the right temperature. If the oven is too hot, the cake may crack and become too small. If the oven is too low, the cake may be wrong in texture and stick to the pan. Overbaking makes for dryness, while not enough baking may cause the cake to fall.

Shortening—For best results have shortening at room temperature. This may be all butter, or butter and margarine or a vegetable shortening combined.

Flour—It is preferable to use cake flour. If, however, all-purpose flour is used, reduce the amount by 2 tablespoons per cup. All-purpose flour, if beaten too long, tends to make cakes tough. Sift flour before measuring.

Eggs—Use fresh eggs if possible. However, eggs three days old give a greater yield than day old eggs.

Most recipes state the desired type of baking powder preferred. Best results come from adhering to these directions.

Flavoring—It is wise to use high grade extracts. They are economical in the long run because of their greater potency.

Use exact ingredients called for—cake flour, double acting baking powder, etc. Bake at temperature and for time indicated. When you wish to line the cake pans with waxed paper, set the pan on a large sheet of paper and cut around the pan with scissors. After cutting out, place paper in bottom of pan. This should fit snugly. Another method is to grease the pan and sprinkle with a little flour; shake out surplus flour by gently knocking pan on hard surface.

By not using the correct amount of ingredients, nor accurate level measurements, nor baking at the right temperature for the right time, you will produce an ordinary cake instead of an exceptional one. When mixing the batter, cream shortening, add eggs—then dry ingredients, alternately with the milk and flavoring. Remember always start by adding flour first, followed by the liquid, to prevent curdling. Do not overmix, as this causes poor texture and reduces volume. When beaten egg whites are used, they are delicately folded in last.

For a single cake, bake on rack in center of oven. For two or three layers, place pans so that they do not touch sides of each other or the oven. (Never place pans directly over each other, as this reduces heat radiation.) If paper is used on the bottom of layer cake pans, remove it from the cake as soon as cake is placed on rack and pan removed—this keeps the paper from sticking to the bottom of the cake. Set heat control on oven about twenty minutes before baking time, to insure an overall temperature of heat.

CAKE MIXES

In this modern day and age, the outstanding flour companies, having spent thousands of dollars in research, have come up with cake mixes which produce excellent cakes. Cupcakes, tube cakes, square, sheet or layer cakes can all be made with cake mixes.

These come in interesting and diversified types; Snowy Angel Food—Golden Yellow Cake—Fluffy White Cake—Gingerbread—Devil's Food—Spice Cake—Marble Cake.

The pans should be the exact size called for in the recipe. Any change in this respect, such as using a larger or smaller pan, or one that is more shallow, may mean failure for the cake.

For white cakes, the metal pans should be bright and shiny, inside and out, to make for even baking and browning. This, however, is not necessary when baking dark cakes such as devil's food, gingerbread, etc. While we consider a pastry brush essential for a cake baker, if you do not have one, you may use a piece of folded paper to apply the thin film of oil or shortening to your pan. When cutting a fresh cake or spreading frosting, occasionally dip the knife in hot water.

FROSTINGS AND ICINGS

When a cake is attractively frosted with a well chosen delicious frosting, it becomes a wonderful treat.

Bear in mind that frosting is always best when used the day it is made, although many frostings keep fresh for a number of days. It is advisable to first frost the cake with a thin, smooth layer of frosting to hold down the crumbs; and after permitting this to set, you will find the final frosting will spread more easily.

Never start to prepare a frosting until you have read the recipe from beginning to end, and be especially fussy about measuring ingredients. However, the amount of extracts or spices may be increased or reduced to suit your own taste.

We find that before using confectioners' sugar it is wise to sift it first, then spoon lightly into measuring cup. If brown sugar is lumpy, roll out lumps with a rolling pin, packing it down with back of spoon until it holds its shape when turned out of cup. When measuring butter or margarine, one fourth pound of butter (one stick) is equal to one half cup or eight tablespoons. To measure two tablespoons, cut in half—then half again—one stick of butter. If you are making an orange frosting, you will find that one medium orange will make one third cup of juice, and the rind of one grated medium orange makes two tablespoons of grated rind.

A fifteen ounce package of raisins makes three cups. (not packed)

One pound of sifted confectioners' sugar makes four cups.

One pound of granulated sugar makes two and one third cups.

One pound of brown sugar makes 2½ to 3 cups, firmly packed.

One medium lemon makes 3 tablespoons of lemon juice, and one tablespoon of grated rind.

Brush loose crumbs from cake and trim any ragged edges with scissors. Use a spatula to spread frosting. Spread sides first, using uphand strokes, then pile frosting on top of the cake and occasionally dip the spatula in a glass of warm water to obtain a smooth and glossy surface.

MOUNTAIN SNOW FROSTING

1¼ cups light corn syrup
⅛ teaspoon salt
2 egg whites
1½ teaspoons vanilla

Bring the corn syrup to a boil. Beat egg whites until soft peaks are formed—add salt. Into this egg mixture gradually pour in syrup. Continue to beat until frosting is fluffy and of a spreading consistency. Add vanilla. This will fill and frost two 8″ layers.

"YUMMY" FUDGE FROSTING

3 squares unsweetened chocolate
2 tablespoons butter
2¾ cups sifted confectioners' sugar
⅛ teaspoon salt
6 tablespoons light cream
2 teaspoons vanilla extract

In double boiler melt and blend chocolate and butter. Add 1¾ cups confectioners' sugar, salt and cream all at one time, and beat thoroughly until smooth. Cook over a low fire until mixture bubbles around the edges. Remove from heat.

Add the remaining sugar in three parts, stirring well after each part is added—add vanilla. Allow it to cool until it is thick enough to spread. This will frost and fill two 8″ layers.

This "yummy" frosting is extremely popular with the younger set and is, comparatively speaking, simple to make.

LUSCIOUS CUSTARD FILLING

2 tablespoons flour
¼ teaspoon salt
⅓ cup granulated sugar
1 egg (beaten lightly)
¾ cup scalded milk
¾ cup heavy cream (whipped)
1½ teaspoons vanilla

Mix dry ingredients in double boiler—add slightly beaten egg—then milk. Mix thoroughly. While constantly stirring, let cook over boiling water for 5 minutes. Let cook for five minutes more, occasionally stirring. Place in refrigerator until cold. Now fold in whipped cream, adding vanilla.

This makes filling for two 9″ layers. Our suggestion is that you make this cake with our famous Snow Flake Icing (recipe on next page).

SNOW FLAKE ICING

1⅓ cups light corn syrup
2 egg whites
⅛ teaspoon salt
1 teaspoon vanilla

Bring corn syrup to boiling point. Beat egg whites until soft flakes are formed, add salt to eggs. Gradually pour syrup over eggs—constantly beating until peaks are formed when lifting beater. Stir in vanilla.

This generously frosts two 9″ layers.

WHITE WILLOW FUDGE FROSTING

1 cup sugar
½ cup + 1 level tablespoon butter
¼ cup light cream
2 cups confectioners' sugar (sifted)
1½ teaspoons vanilla

Melt butter, gradually adding sugar, then cream, stir thoroughly. Occasionally stir until this mixture boils. Let cool, then add confectioners' sugar until frosting is of spreading consistency. Add vanilla.

Note: This white fudge frosting is excellent for dark cake, i.e. devil's food, chocolate chip, or marble cake.

MOCHA BUTTER FROSTING

This is made with strong, fresh coffee infusion.

½ cup cold strong coffee
1 cup cold water
¼ cup soft butter
2 cups + confectioners' sugar
¼ teaspoon salt
1 tablespoon corn syrup

Make sure coffee is clear and no grounds are included. Add water to coffee, heat just to the boiling point. Remove from stove, allow to cool.

Cream butter well and add sugar gradually, alternating with three tablespoons of coffee. Add salt and corn syrup until this mixture is of spreading consistency.

This may be used for any type of cake, and is especially delicious. It is a good base for nuts and fruits. These may be added to the frosting; two tablespoons each of chopped pecans and candied cherries.

DARK CHOCOLATE FROSTING

1½ cups confectioners' sugar
⅓ cup good cocoa
¼ cup soft butter
3 tablespoons cream
1 teaspoon vanilla

Measure required amount of sugar after sifting first. Then sift sugar and cocoa together. In saucepan cream butter until very soft, add sugar and cocoa mixture alternately with cream, stirring thoroughly. Place over low heat until spreading consistency. Stir in vanilla thoroughly. This makes a glossy, dark and smooth frosting which spreads beautifully on the cake.

1959
HAPPY
1960
NEW
YEAR

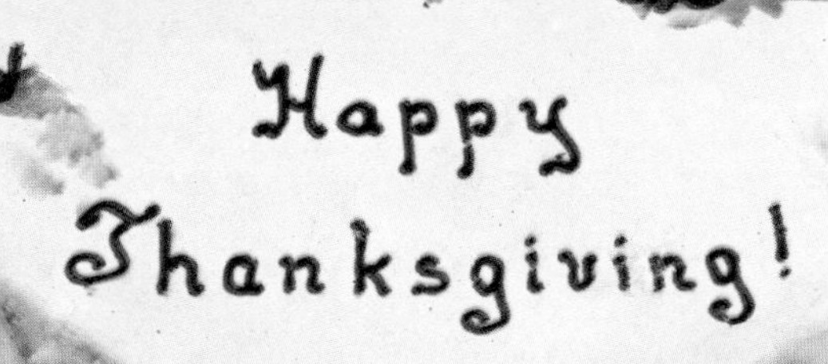

Wouldn't this cake make your Thanksgiving dinner a festive occasion?
The chrysanthemums are made with tube No. 80.

It's so easy to make this Christmas cake —
the frosted cardboard base gives you plenty of room
to say "Merry Christmas."

The youngster's birthday party would be a tremendous success
with this carnival cake.

To the girl who is taking dancing lessons,
the ballerina cake would make her party complete.

ASTER TUBES (CROSS TUBES)

Asters come in pink, white, violet or purple. The smallest tube used for these is No. 49. The aster tubes come in six sizes and can also be used for writing, lettering and the making of small buds.

No. 53 shows an exceptionally simple scroll, good for beginners. No. 54 shows another good design. You may pipe two parallel lines, and with tube No. 1 and contrasting colors, you may pipe the threads and join both lines.

No. 54 also make a large aster. To make an aster slant, pipe twelve or fourteen pointed petals in a circle flat on the cake; continue by piping twelve or fourteen more petals in between the first row. By drawing the hand slightly upward put in a third row of petals, slightly shorter. Gradually draw each petal a little more vertically until center petals appear to be standing up straight. Use your judgement as to the fullness of the flower, as some asters are fuller than others.

OVAL TUBES

These tubes are used for any work done where the half-round effect is desired, and they make interesting scrolls, various flowers, stems, etc. Oval tubes are Nos. 55 to 58 inclusive.

As you will note on picture, tube No. 55 where the lines meet, there is a bead piped on each point, with plain tube No. 3. For contrast and beauty, it is suggested you make these beads in a different color.

The Easter Lily is an easy flower to make and is always done in white butter cream. As you will observe on page 38, using tube No. 57, make narrow petals at the start, gradually widening by more pressure on the bag, then tapering to a nice point at the end.

Begin by piping one petal flat on the cake, drawing up the point just a bit. Then form two petals, each partly on top of the first petal—one on the right, and one on the left. Draw each petal to the side a trifle to permit the point of the first petal to be visible. Now add two more slightly longer petals with the points turning more sharply to each side. Finally pipe one last petal in between the previous two, making this a bit larger than the others with its point turned straight up.

With plain tube No. 1, make four yellow dots in the center of the petal. The lower part of the petals should be colored pale green. We suggest a fine paint brush for this. The stem of the lily is made with plain tube No. 3, and with leaf tube No. 66, make several attractive leaves. These little motifs may be used to decorate petit-fours on French pastry.

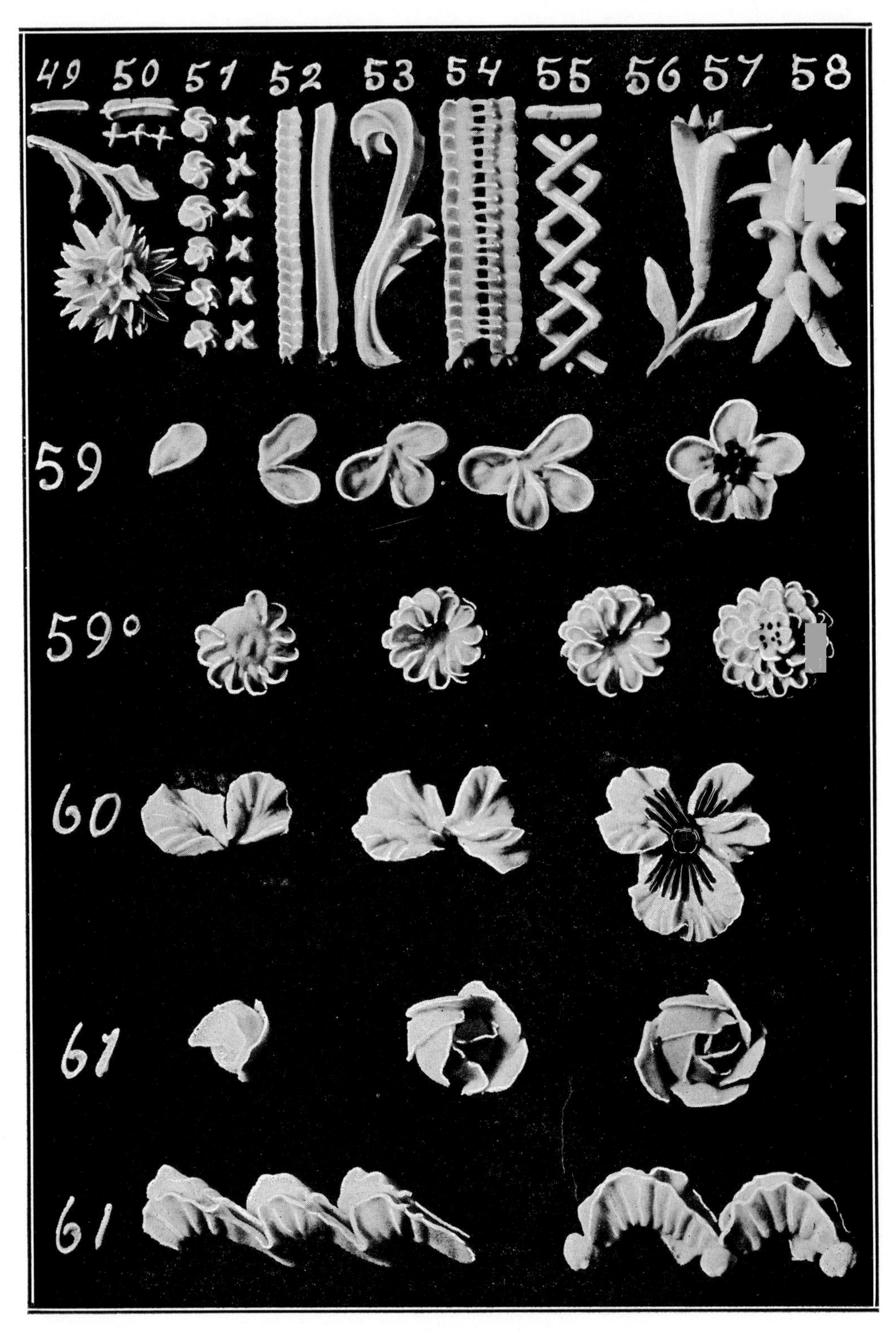

Number indicates tube used to make design.

FLOWER TUBES

No. 59. Periwinkles and apple blossoms are very similar in shape and size but, as you know, the colors are entirely different. The periwinkle is a deep purplish blue. This color is acquired by using butter cream to which blue coloring has been added in sufficient quantity to make the shade quite deep. Now add a small amount of red coloring, alternating between red and blue, but bear in mind that a periwinkle is more blue than purple. Nevertheless, the red adds a tone of beauty to the mixture.

APPLE BLOSSOM

On page 59 you will find directions and illustrations of the apple blossom, given in step by step progression.

No. 59°. The dahlia is shown with each progressive step on page 58, with complete instructions (see corresponding number on plate with complete illustrations).

No. 60. This is primarily a pansy tube, although we also use much larger tubes to make this flower. There are many varieties of the pansy. Some, you will find, have three petals at the top and two at the bottom, and many vice versa.

No. 61. This versatile little tube can be used for making the small rose; it is also useful for making the open or wild rose.

FANCY BORDER TUBES (THREE SIZES)

All decorated cakes, regardless of how elaborate or simple they may be, have a finishing touch we call the border. These borders are made in many sizes, and are supposed to complement the cake. There is a choice of where these borders may be placed. We usually place an attractive border at the base, but in large wedding cakes a border is used at the base of the bottom tier, and a corresponding one at the outer edge of the disk.

No. 63. This tube is a bit smaller than tube No. 62 (see an interesting border made with this tube on page 40). You will note that this border is finished with a wavy piping just below the last ridge on the flat line.

No. 64. This border is made by holding the tube practically flat on the cake. Move slowly from side to side. This pipes a crinkled line. On top of this, pipe a flat even line just below the ridge. Now hold the tube at a slight angle and pipe one more line over the preceding two, making it stand up, slightly tilted. As you will see in the illustration, the two lines are shown only half finished, in order to make it clear as to how these two lines are piped.

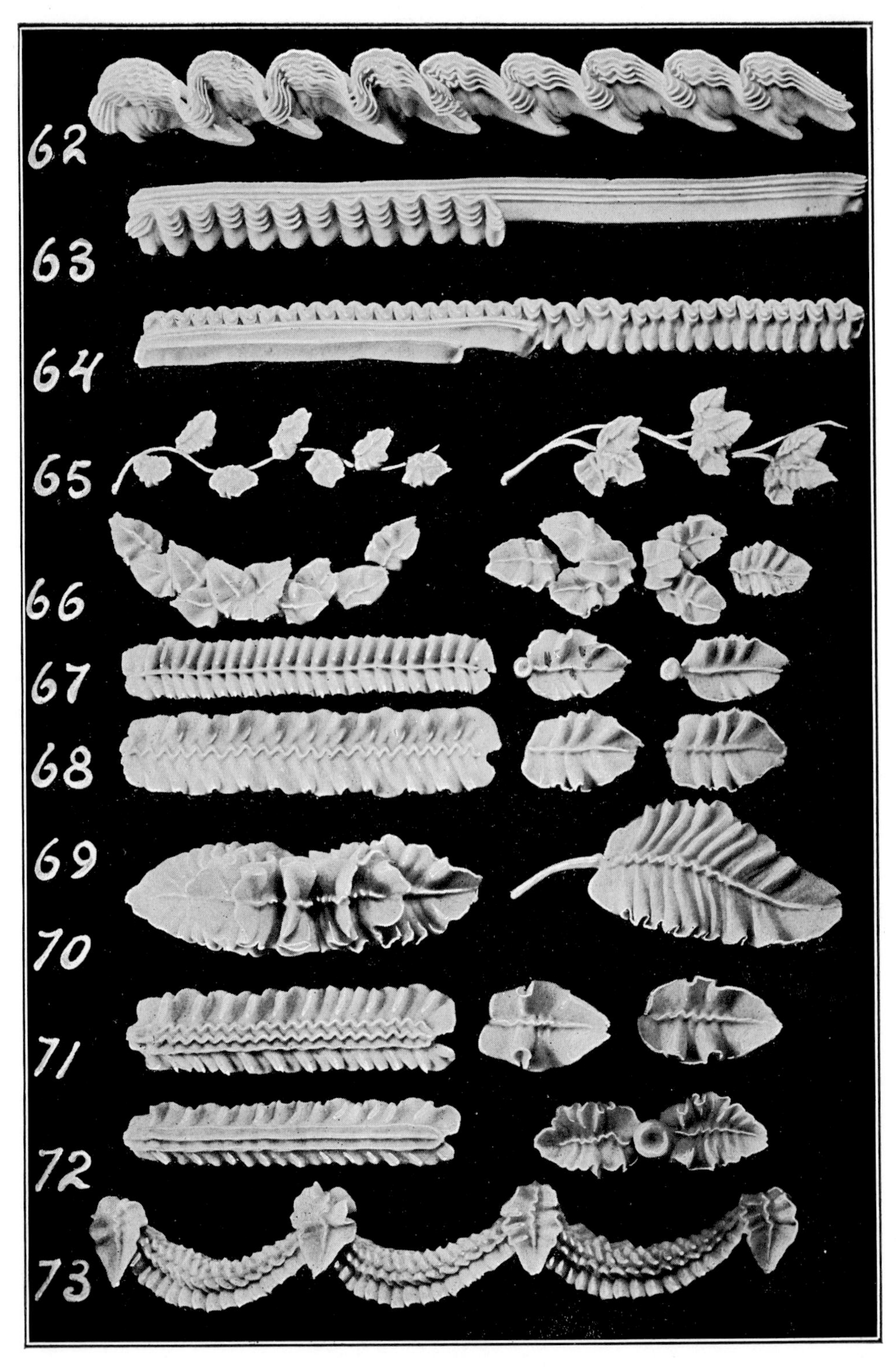

Number indicates tube used to make design.

LEAF TUBES (SIX SIZES)

Leaf tubes are Nos. 65 to 70 inclusive. For tiny leaves use tube No. 65. In the illustration we show small leaves on a stem and clusters of leaves on stems attached to a branch.

In making larger leaves (with tubes Nos. 68, 69, 70) we suggest the tube be held in an almost perpendicular position to create a standing leaf. Place tube on cake behind a petal of the flower, then exert considerable pressure of your hand on the bag, draw it up very slowly, continuing pressure and making a point at the end of the leaf as you break away. If a split occurs at this point pinch it together gently with fingers. When making a leaf for a red or pink rose, prepare butter cream as follows: Spread pale green on your table, using an adequate amount to fill bag. Place a blot of red coloring on the board with the tip of the spatula (after dipping in red coloring) and make eight or ten small dots in three rows from top to bottom. Fold the butter cream over carefully so as not to mix. This is done to create an interesting red vein running through the green leaf. This makes for as near nature's handiwork as possible.

COMBINATION LEAF AND BORDER TUBES

No. 71. If you examine this tube, you will see that it is different on each side.
To make a leaf as in illustration, turn the seam upward. A very fine border may be made by turning the seam down. This border is made with a side to side wavy motion. Note these uneven center lines. With a No. 1 or No. 2 tube, you may, using a different color icing, go over these lines, creating an interesting contrast.
There is shown a picture of two leaves made this way, by having the center seam on top. This forms an attractive leaf as it has a distinct ridge down the center.

No. 72. Is a smaller replica of the above design. We suggest when this tube is used for a border that the center line be made straight with a complimentary color. There are also shown two crinkled leaves, which are made into an interesting motif by linking together with a circlet made with plain tube No. 2.

No. 73. The smallest of these three interesting tubes is generally used for a fine garland border. The scallops of these garlands are joined by the leaf motif made by using the other side of the tube.
We suggest you use a pale green icing for the leaf and any pastel shade of your choice for the border.

No. 74. (Large size.) Here we offer another interesting combination tube with a different design on each side. By making a side to side wavy

Number indicates tube used to make design.

COMBINATION TUBES

motion, and the seam of the tube toward the cake, the design will resemble fluting. By turning the tube around, using the same motion, a tiny crinkly design will appear, resembling gathers. Many borders are similar in design to beautiful hand embroidery work.

No. 75. (Medium size.) This is exactly the same tube, but one size smaller. Therefore, it lends itself to a rather unusual border, using No. 1 tube for the thread work. Now by turning tube directly around a straight line may be drawn, but you will see that this tube makes a series of straight lines, as shown in illustration.

No. 76. This little versatile tube, although the same in make and design, is used in delightful little scallops which furnish a lane for a contrasting color.

No. 78. This tube is used primarily to make phantasy flowers, which are more definite little buds, the centers of which may be filled with color. This may also be used to make delicate borders, by holding at an angle, or if preferred, in a vertical position.

FLOWER TUBES

No. 79. This tube, also tubes Nos. 80 and 81, are used to create daffodils, narcissus, lilies of the valley and a group of phantasy flowers, etc.

In the illustration on page 42, you see two straight lines—the upper one being concave, made by holding the seam of the tube toward the cake. The lower line is made by holding the tube in reverse position, thus making a convex line.

These two lines may be used to make a real attractive border design simply and quickly. Make a border of convex lines and fill with piped thread work, using a No. 2 plain tube and complimentary colors.

No. 80. The first illustration shows a phantasy flower. Pipe six petals from the center as shown with a white icing. Using No. 2 plain tube and with a red icing, pipe a ring in the center, completing the flower.

No. 81. To the right, in the illustration, a daffodil is made. Use a light yellow icing to make the cup. Then with a much deeper shade of yellow icing, make six petals. Start these petals narrow and gradually widen by applying more pressure to the cone, decreasing to a graceful tapered point.

After piping, with tube No. 2 and pale green icing, complete by adding two or three graceful leaves to the stem.

Make a yellow stamen by inserting tube No. 1 and yellow icing directly into the center of the cup. By using an upward motion and breaking off quickly, you will have a natural looking flower.

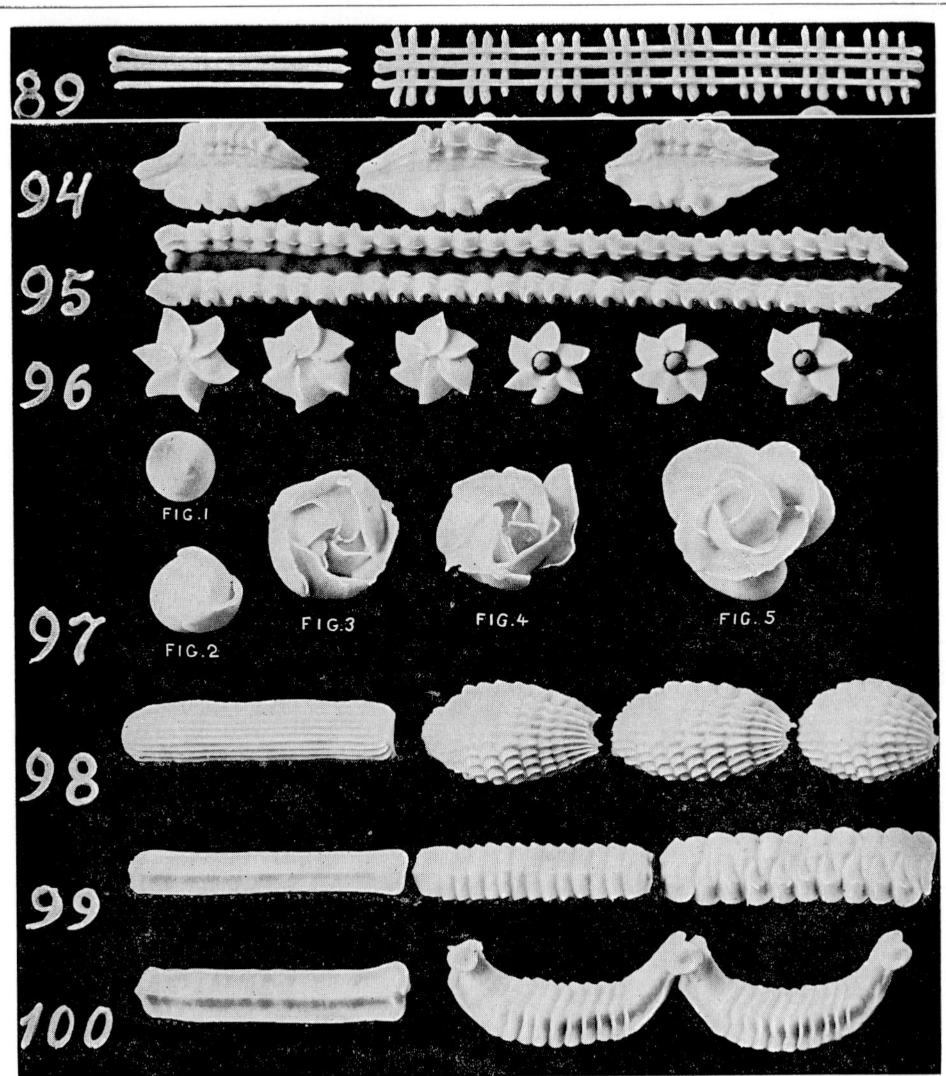

Number indicates tube used to make design.

These illustrations are reproductions of cake tops decorated with plain and star tubes. Designs such as these are easy to make and are ideal suggestions for the beginner.

SQUARE TUBES (Concave Sides)

The two square lines are made with tube No. 82 and decorated with beads made with the square tubes.

They complement the cake when used for a border—on the extreme edge. The scallops in the illustration are made with the smaller tubes (Nos. 83 and 84) finished with a dot between each scallop.

No. 85. These curved lines and triangular beads are made with this tube. In fact, everything accomplished with tubes Nos. 82, 83 and 84 may be made with this unusual triangular tube.

BORDER TUBES NOS. 86–87–88

With an up and down motion of the hand, you will soon, with a little practice, be able to make these most outstanding of all borders. They are versatile in type, and permit the user to originate his very own designs.

May we stress the need for complete study of the illustrations, as they indicate the many uses and designs to be made.

In illustration No. 88, using tube No. 2 or 3, make the distinctive circlet between each scallop.

TRIPLE LINE TUBE

No. 89. This we call our weaving tube. It is preferred by beginners for basket work, because the parallel lines can be made in one operation.

FRENCH LEAF TUBES NOS. 94 AND 95

These tubes are used especially for intricate fern work and borders and various special leaves. No. 94 is the smaller of the two and used for more delicate work.

DROP FLOWER TUBE

No. 96. With a slight press of the bag, an individual flower appears. Before releasing, give one tiny push forward making a distinct indentation, allowing this to be filled with contrasting color.

FULL BLOOM ROSE TUBE

No. 97. By looking closely at your illustration of this tube, you will find the beginning of the rose is made by using a small dome as shown in Fig. 1. Fig. 2 shows that the second row of petals is made very close to this dome. This is done by holding the bag in a vertical position, Fig. 3. Gradually as you progress with other petals, allow the bag to be used in a more horizontal position, showing the rose opening, as in full bloom.

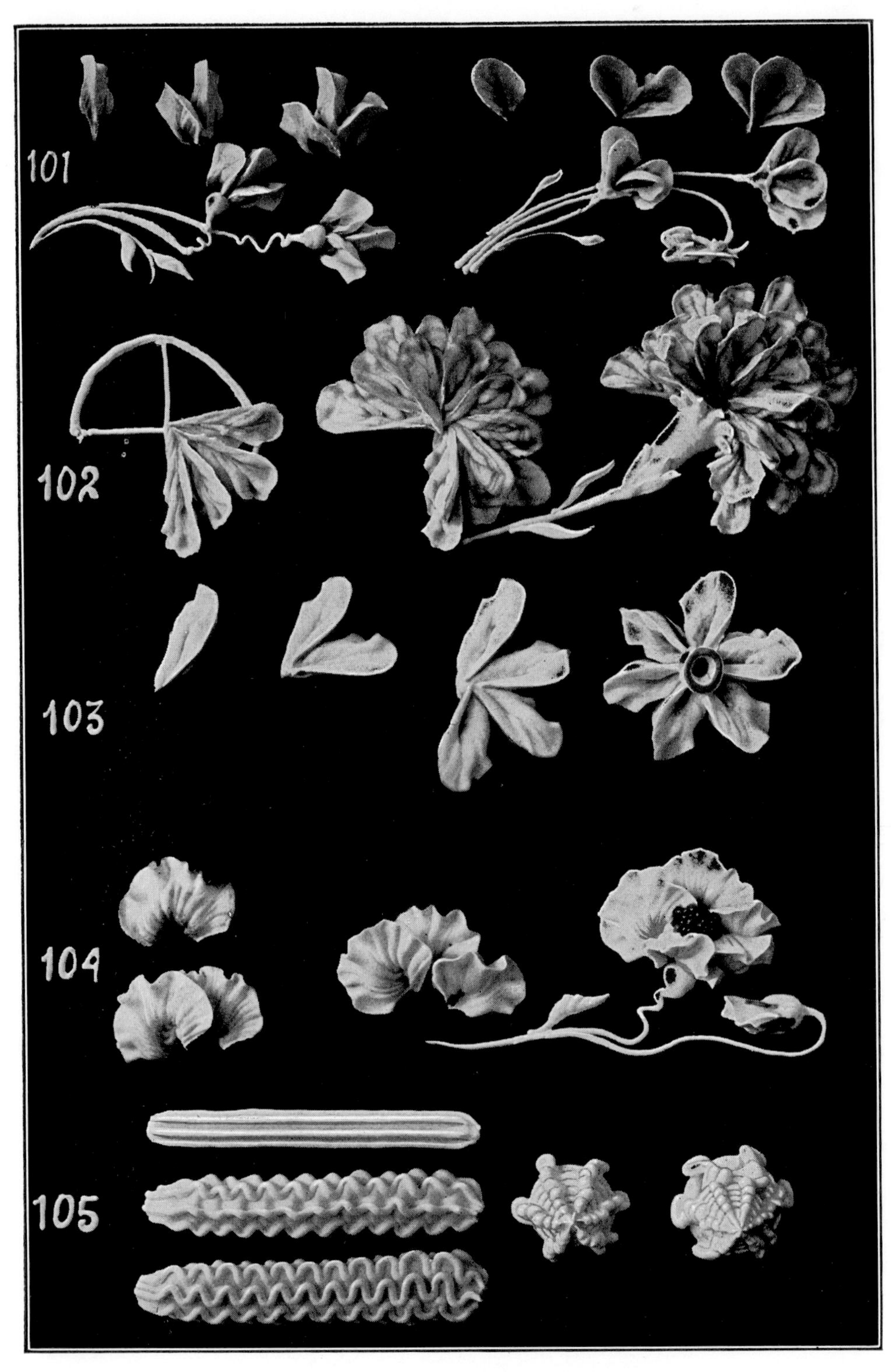

Number indicates tube used to make design.

SHELL TUBE

No. 98. This is an interesting little shell tube and is a perfect dandy for centers and many other decorations. It produces a shell-like design and may be used individually or joined together to form a border.

SPECIAL BORDER AND GARLAND TUBES

No. 99. If you study the illustration, you will find the three distinct designs that may be accomplished with this tube. For instance: By holding bag perpendicularly and with a steady hand, a straight line may be made. By using an up and down wavy motion, you will produce a wavy border. A side to side wavy motion creates a more important looking border for a larger cake.

No. 100. There is a marked similarity of tubes Nos. 99 and 100, but tube No. 100, being larger, is used primarily for borders and wavy garlands. These may be finished by making small circles with tube No. 2 between each scallop. To complement the decoration of your cake, a contrasting color may be used.

FLOWER TUBES

No. 101. Makes sweet peas and violets. On pages 64 and 65 you will find complete instructions, as well as further illustrations for making these flowers.

No. 102. The illustration shows a carnation. Detailed instructions are on page 66.

No. 103. Shows the narcissus. See page 68 for instructions.

No. 104. Is used for the poppy and small roses. See page 69 for poppy, and page 63 for the roses.

OVERPIPING BORDER TUBES

No. 105. The illustration on the opposite page shows three ideal borders. The first was made by holding tube at an angle and drawing out in a straight line. The second was made with a slight up and down wavy motion, and a side to side wavy motion was used for the third.

This tube can also be used for candies, petit fours and butter patties, as shown in the last two designs.

FRENCH PASTRIES

One of the most popular desserts is the French Pastry, so called to differentiate from the pastries of other countries. This definitely has a value of its own, due to the fact that it lends itself to beautiful decorations, which are a distinct asset to the hostess desiring her dessert table to be one of unique beauty. Among these dessert specialities are Napoleons, filled patty shells, creamed horns. and apple turnovers.

We believe it wise for the beginner to learn to make a good puff pastry. The following recipe is for "chow" pastry. It is always used for puffs and eclairs, and we believe it is one of the finest recipes you will ever receive.

CHOW PASTRY

½ cup butter
1 cup boiling water
1 cup sifted enriched flour
½ teaspoon salt
4 eggs

Melt ½ cup of butter in the cup of boiling water, place in a saucepan. Add the flour sifted with salt all at once to liquid ingredients, stirring constantly. Cook this until mixture leaves the sides of the pan in a smooth ball. Remove from heat and cool for about one minute. Add eggs, beating vigorously after each egg is added, until the mixture becomes smooth and shiny. Drop by full rounded teaspoons on lightly greased cookie sheet and bake in hot oven 400° F. until golden brown (about 18 minutes). Makes 24 puffs.

Now we are going to give you a few interesting fillings from our famous collection.

LEMON COCONUT CREAM

1 cup + 1 tablespoon powdered sugar
2 egg yolks (slightly beaten)
Grated rind 1½ lemons
Juice 1½ lemons
1 cup shredded coconut

Put sugar in bowl, add egg yolks, rind and lemon juice. Stir constantly while cooking in double boiler—approximately 10 minutes—now add coconut.

BUTTERSCOTCH FILLING

4 tablespoons butter
¾ cup brown sugar
2 cups light cream
⅓ cup flour
½ teaspoon salt
2 slightly beaten eggs
½ teaspoon vanilla

Put butter in saucepan, blend in sugar, and cook about two minutes—until syrup starts to turn brown. Add 1½ cups cream, scald over hot water. To the flour and salt mixture add remaining ½ cup of cream, add to hot mixture and cook about 15 minutes. Lastly, add eggs to this mixture and cook 2 minutes. Cool slightly before adding vanilla.

WHIPPED CREAM CHOCOLATE FILLING

2 tablespoons butter
4 oz. unsweetened chocolate
½ pint heavy cream
2 cups 10X confectioners' sugar

After melting butter and chocolate, cool slightly and add cream and sugar. Beat until thick and smooth. Add ½ cup chopped pecans or walnuts if desired.

COFFEE CREAM FILLING

½ pint heavy cream
¼ cup confectioners' sugar
1 egg white
½ teaspoon vanilla
⅛ teaspoon salt

After beating cream until stiff, add sugar slowly. Fold in stiffly beaten egg white, salt and vanilla. Now add strong coffee drop by drop until the desired coffee flavor is reached.

These fillings are very versatile. They may be used for puffs, tarts, pies and to make interesting fillings between the layers of cakes.

PEPPERMINT CREAM PUFFS

½ lb. peppermint stick candy (thoroughly crushed)
2 cups heavy cream
½ tablespoon unflavored gelatin
1 tablespoon cold water

Cook crushed peppermint candy and ½ cup of heavy cream in double boiler until candy is dissolved, using very low heat. Dissolve ½ tablespoon gelatin in 1 tablespoon cold water. Pour into the peppermint mixture and cook a few minutes. After whipping the balance of the cream, fold it gently into the mixture. Using the large tube (No. 8) and your pastry bag, fill approximately 12 large or 18 small puffs.

To attractively decorate these filled puffs and make them still more delicious, use a good chocolate icing and star tube No. 16 and make a shell motif. To make these, hold bag at a sharp angle, and squeeze a bit of icing from the tube, release pressure, bring tube to a vertical position. These shells are made more beautiful by bringing bag to a point.

EMERALD ISLE FILLING FOR TARTS

Make tart shells (about 12 large or 18 small), using your favorite pie pastry. Fill these with the following delicate green filling, and trim with dark green gum drops, piped with border of whipped cream.

3 eggs (separated)
1 cup granulated sugar
½ cup lemon juice
⅓ teaspoon salt
1 tablespoon grated lemon rind

1 envelope unflavored gelatin
¼ cup cold water
large green gum drops
1 cup heavy whipped cream

After beating egg yolks, put in top of double boiler, add ⅔ cup sugar, lemon juice and ⅓ teaspoon salt. Cook over hot water until slightly thickened, stirring constantly; remove from heat. Beat egg whites stiffly (but not dry). Gradually beat in the balance of the sugar (⅓ cup) and 1 tablespoon lemon rind. Stir in gelatin dissolved in water, and add a few drops of green vegetable coloring. Chill until partially thickened. Pile into the baked tart shells. Chill and decorate with cut dark green gum drops. Surround this with little phantasy flowers made with star tube No. 16. These are a real party dessert, delicately sweet, and as pretty as a flower.

PETITS FOURS

Petits Fours for the dessert tray are tiny cakes which add exquisite beauty to the sweet table, and when properly made and decorated, will appeal to the most discerning gourmet.

Bake sheets of rich butter sponge cake—cool, and cut into divider strips and sandwich together with extra butter cream or your favorite jelly. Cut with fancy cutters, such as star, heart, crescent, diamond, clover leaf, half moon, triangles. By having cutters sharp, and occasionally dipping them in water, you will avoid ragged edges and surface crumbling. Frost top and sides with boiled icing. Do not fail to place them in attractive fluted cups and put in refrigerator to set the icing.

These little cakes may be decorated to your choice. Here is where the decorating tubes come into play. The half moons are decorated with tube No. 19, piping a crinkled border completely around edge. On the oblong cakes, it is nice to make baby apple blossoms and narcissus with tube No. 104. Use tube No. 2 to pipe the stems and tube No. 1 to make little "stand up" stamens. If you want to lend a touch of humor to the petits fours tray, make a pair of dice by first icing little cubes of cake about 1 cubic inch. Ice these with white boiled icing and use tube No. 3 to make the spots on the dice.

On chocolate iced cakes, pale green and pink, or green and yellow may be used for a fine effect.

PRACTICAL SUGGESTIONS

Never let icing harden in tubes; drop them into a glass of water. Cleanse thoroughly when work is completed. This may be done quickly by holding under a stream of water.

Always beat the icing well, as continuous brisk beating makes it more pliable, clearer and much whiter. (We always suggest this when making white roses, and lilies of the valley.)

The utensils used in making icings must be scrupulously clean and free from grease.

When sifting confectioners' sugar—(and sift you *must*), use a special fine mesh sieve and keep only for this purpose, thus eliminating any foreign ingredients, i.e. flour, starch, etc.

X

ROYAL ICING

1 lb. (3⅓ cups) sifted confectioners' sugar
½ teaspoon cream of tartar
3 egg whites, unbeaten
½ teaspoon vanilla

After combining all ingredients in the electric mixer, beat at low speed until sugar is dissolved. Turn indicator to high speed until mixture is light and fluffy.
Keep icing covered with damp cloth. When using the fine tubes with small, narrow openings, a little egg white may be added if the icing has become too stiff.

X

BUTTER CREAM ICING

There are many recipes for this most versatile and tasty of all decorating icings. It can be used for decorating as well as frostings and fillings.
Here is a basic formula for Butter Cream Icing.

¼ cup butter or margarine
speck salt
2 cups sifted confectioners' sugar
3 tablespoons milk or light cream
¼ teaspoon vanilla

After whipping the shortening at high speed until it is fluffy, gradually add 1 cup sugar and reduce to low speed, add liquid, salt and flavoring, then the balance of the sugar. It is possible to control the consistency of this icing simply by adding a bit more sugar for a firmer icing, or a little more liquid for a softer icing.

For chocolate butter icing add ½ oz. melted chocolate to above.
The yolk of one egg will make yellow icing.
Strong coffee instead of milk will make Mocha icing.
Using, of course, only one flavor at a time.

ATECO DECORATING COMB

This little gadget is a must in the decorator's kitchen. It is made of strong aluminum and will not bend and may be used on Butter Cream icing, Whipped cream, Meringue, Mashed potatoes, Cheese Spreads, etc.

We call this our little time saver. It may be used quickly, and produces a professional, finished look.

COLORED ICING

To obtain the best results, it is advisable to mix colors in the daylight, as the artificial light changes the tone of the colors completely.

There are four basic vegetable colors—Red, Blue, Yellow and Green. From these it is possible to make any desired shade.

Following is a list of combinations which make the different colors.

Red and Yellow . . . . Orange

Red and Blue . . . . Violet or Purple

Yellow and Blue . . . . Green

Green and Red . . . . Brown

Be cautious in mixing the colors, adding a tiny bit at a time, as it tends to deepen in shade within a half hour after mixing.

Flowers and fruits are seldom made as dark as nature's colors. We believe it in good taste to keep the colors pastel in shade.

Valentine cake — the small hearts are paper, but the flowers are icing.

Certainly a decorated cake for the youngster's birthday is a 'must'. Here's just one of many ideas that can be used.

Here's a general occasion cake
where the frosting is scalloped with a decorating comb,
then decorated on top.

This Baby Shower cake uses a china stork,
but the bootees nestled in with the petite flowers are icing.

FLOWER NAILS

There are many decorators who prefer making their individual flowers on a nail, instead of directly on the cake. These nails enable you to shape the petals better, thus building up a much more attractive flower.

Before using the flowers nails. they should be waxed with ordinary paraffin so that the flowers may be removed without breaking.

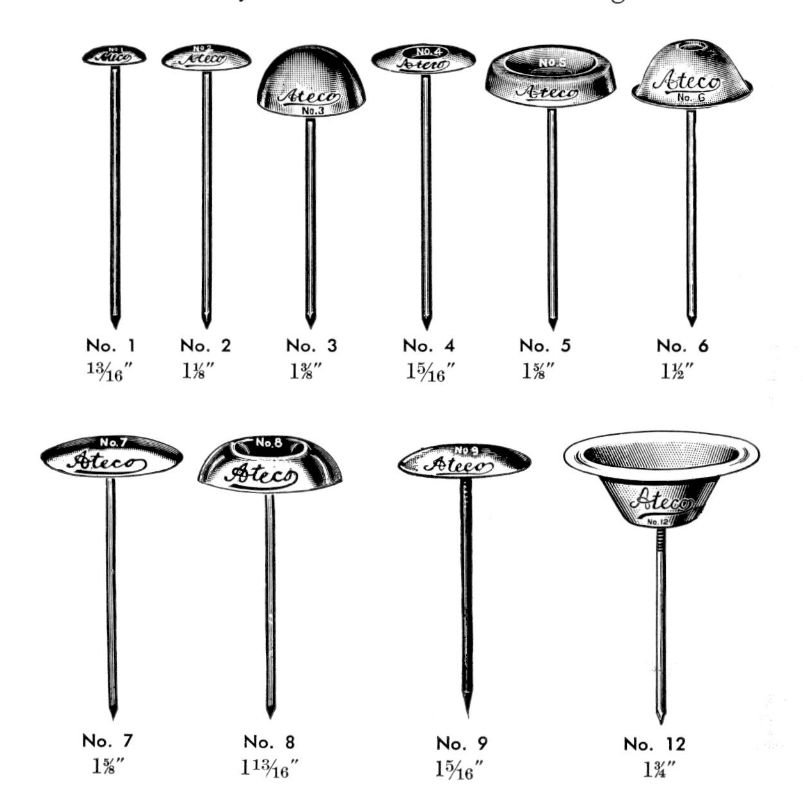

USES OF ATECO FLOWER NAILS

No. 1. For small roses.

No. 2. For violets and small roses.

No. 3. For dahlias and similar flowers.

No. 4. Small daisies and similar petal flowers.

No. 5. For apple blossom or pansy.

No. 6. Peonies.

No. 7. Carnation, daisy, apple blossom, poppy, wild rose, pansy, jonquil, rose, orange blossom, narcissus.

No. 8. Narcissus

No. 9. Rose

No. 12. For Easter Lily, Lilies must harden completely before removing from the nail, so several nails are needed for making many flowers. On the following page you will find illustrations for making:—

Fig. 1. Dahlia

Fig. 2. Apple blossom

Fig. 3. Phantasy flower

Fig. 4. Pansy

Fig. 5. First progressive step of the rose

Fig. 6. Second progressive step of the rose

Fig. 7. Third progressive step of the rose

Fig. 8. Shows the phantasy flower being made flat on the cake using the decorating syringe.

It is the purpose of these illustrations to give you an idea of the way the tube and flower nail should be held while making these flowers.

These illustrations are reproductions of cake tops decorated with plain and star tubes. Designs such as these are easy to make and are ideal suggestions for the beginner.

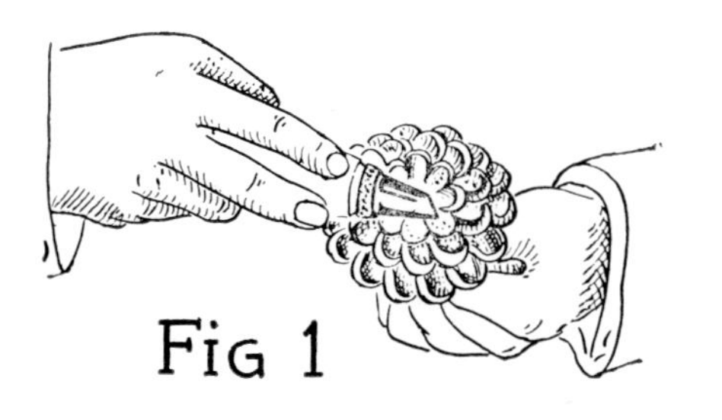
FIG 1

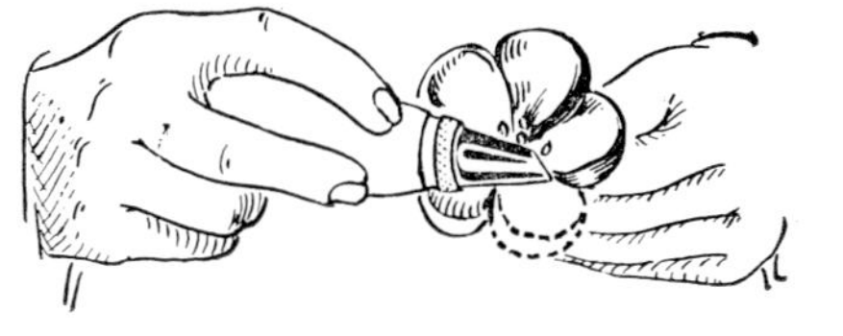
FIG 2

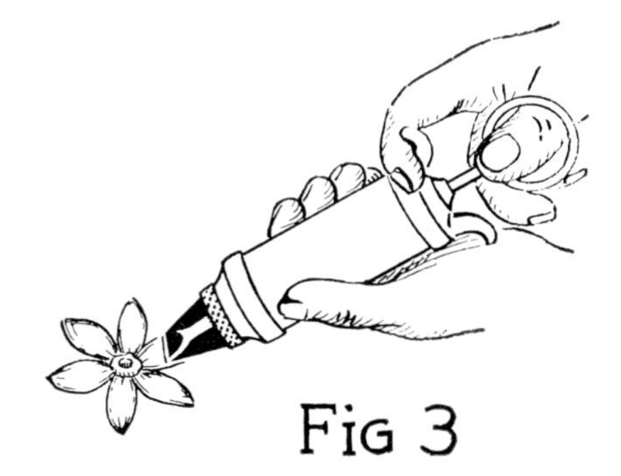
FIG 3

FIG 4

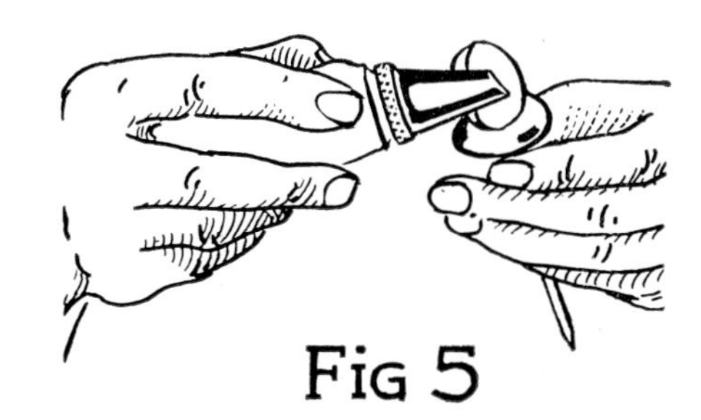
FIG 5

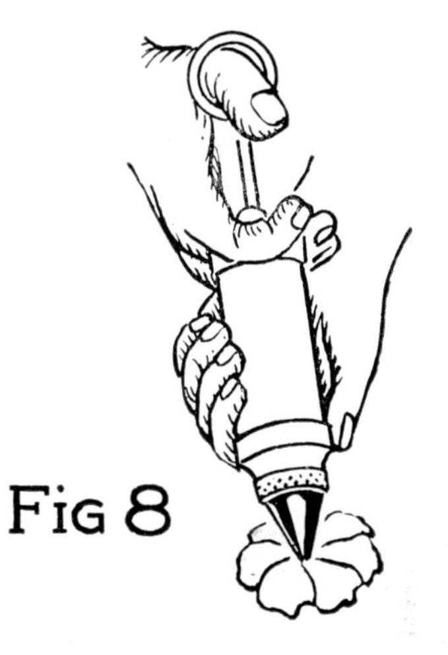
FIG 8

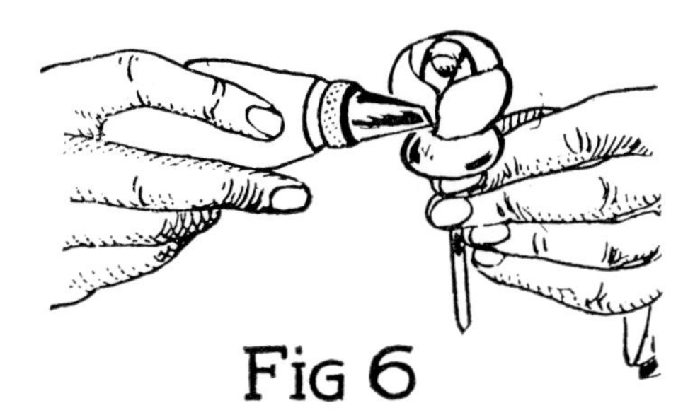
FIG 6

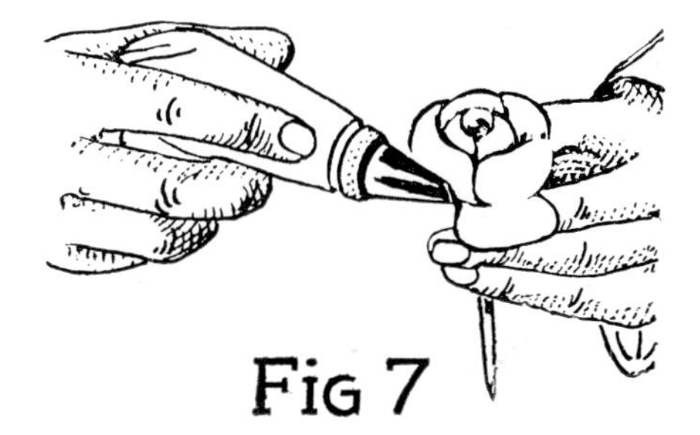
FIG 7

DAHLIAS

The dahlia is made with tube No. 59° in the following manner:

Dahlias come either yellow, orange, deep red, and many times are two-toned in color. The darker shade should be placed at the thin end of the tube.

On a No. 3 flower nail, start the first circle of petals around the outer edge of the nail head. These petals should be of considerable size, as each following row is made smaller than the previous one.

The petals of the second row should be partly over-lapping, and made between the petals of the preceding row.

The petals of the third circle are made the same way as the former one, only a little smaller and nearer to the center.

Continue the last row until the entire flower has been filled in with small petals.

To give a nice finishing touch to the dahlias, use the No. 3 tube and place a few yellow dots in the center.

The proper position for holding the flower nail and tube is illustrated in Fig. 1 on page 57.

APPLE BLOSSOMS

These easy-to-make flowers are made with tube No. 59 in the following manner:

Make the stem of the flower first, with plain tube No. 2, using a brownish-green icing.

Apple blossoms are made with a delicate pink or white icing. Many of these beautiful little flowers also come in two tones of pink. Have the deeper color on the wide side of the tube.

Fig. 2 on page 57 shows the last petal being made on flower nail No. 5.

Finish the center with five dark brown dots.

Since it is desirable to have these blossoms as natural looking as possible, some of them should be slightly tilted. This is done by placing a dot of icing beneath the flower.

ASTERS

Tube No. 50 is used to make the Aster in the following manner:

Make a circle by placing twelve or fourteen pointed petals on the cake.

Pipe ten or twelve more petals in between the first twelve.

By holding the hand slightly perpendicular, pipe a third row of petals a trifle shorter than the preceding row. Continue to pipe petals, having the center ones stand up straight.

These flowers come in the magnificent shades of violet, pink, purple or white. Delightful effects may be produced by enhancing the colors from pale tones to deeper ones.

PANSIES

The pansy is made with tube No. 60 (using bent in part of the tube on the outside). In the following illustrations you will see the three progressive steps in making this lovely flower.

Pansies may be made in almost any color. However, yellow and purple are more often desired. When combining contrasting shades, be sure to remember the color balance.

Using a No. 5 flower nail, with tube No. 60 make the first two petals as illustrated, using a slight wavy motion, so that the petals crinkle a bit.

Make two petals directly below those previously made. Overlap these petals slightly. See Fig. 4 on page 57.

The last petal is considerably larger than the others and should be made with one broad sweep of the wrist.

When flower is completed and dry, dip a #1 paint brush (or use a toothpick) into the clear, pure coloring and stripe the petals with red or blue. The definite lines give depth and character to the pansy.

Make a long, narrow indentation in center of flower and again using paint brush or toothpick, cover completely the edge of the opening with pure yellow. This makes for a professionally completed flower.

When possible, have a real flower beside you which you may study for form and coloring. By placing pansies around in small groups, the varied colors of these flowers will have an ideal effect on your decorated cake.

ORCHID

Because the orchid is made in six sections and then put together, it must be made of royal icing. Stripe one side of a large decorating bag with purple paste color. Fill the remainder of the bag with a delicate purple icing.

Using a No. 124 Special Rose Tube, make the large outside petals. These are made on waxed paper with the large side of the tube touching the paper. The tube is moved up on one side about two inches and then brought down on the other side while maintaining a back and forth motion to create an uneven edge on the outside of the petal. Two of these petals must be made for each orchid. After making 2 of them in a row, lay the waxed paper over a long roll of about an inch in diameter to give the petals a curved effect.

The long narrow petals are made in the same manner. There are three to each orchid and 3 should be made on a sheet. In making these petals, an even steady pressure must be maintained while moving the tube along. These are placed over a long roll in the same manner as the first petals.

The most difficult part of the orchid is making the center which has a sort of inverted cone shape. This is the main section of the orchid. To make the center, a No. 2 Lady Lock Stick should be used. It is held in a down position and the first part of the center petal is started from the rear of the stick about half way up. After the first half of the petal is completed, turn the stick around and start the second half. As the tube is moved down to the bottom of the stick, a slight back and forth motion must be maintained to create an uneven effect. After working around the stick, the opening in the back must be filled in by simply squeezing and moving the tube over it. The rough area can be smoothed out by dipping the forefinger in water and running it over the back of the rough area.

To store for drying, place the Lady Lock Stick over a small bottle such as a pop bottle. This allows the air to dry and harden the petal in about 24 hours.

To assemble the orchid, a small amount of royal icing is piped on waxed paper or directly on the cake. The center of the orchid (the part around the Lady Lock Stick) is placed into the mound standing upright. The two larger petals are placed slightly to the front. Then the three narrower petals are put in place, finishing the flower.

SPECIAL FLOWER TUBES

These special large tubes are used for making large roses and other large flowers. Three styles are illustrated and each style is made in four sizes, making a total of twelve tubes.

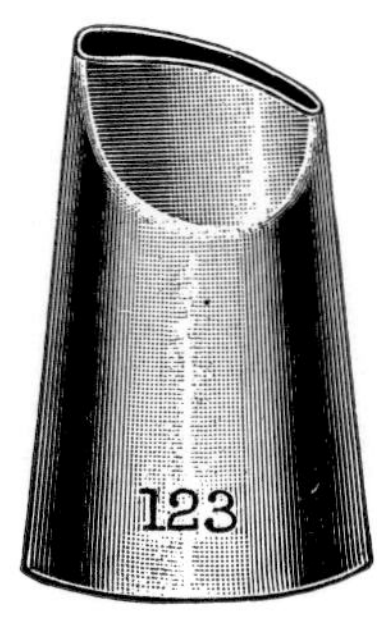

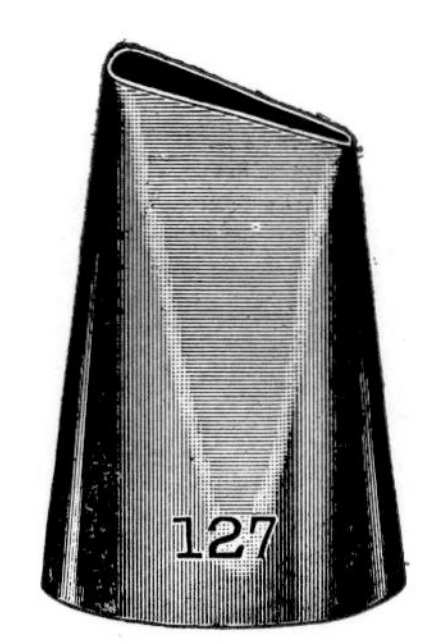

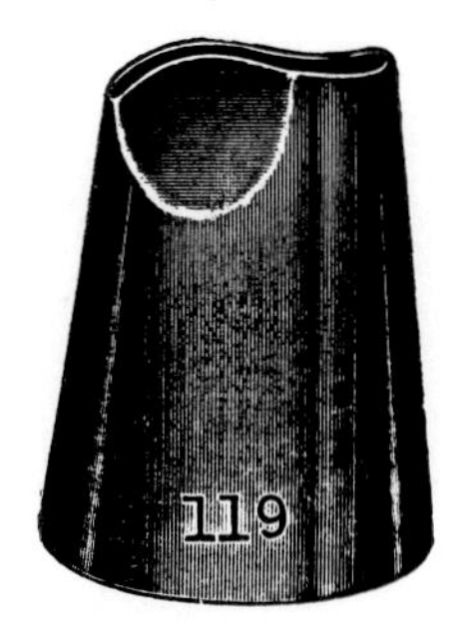

The rose can be made with any of the above tubes, it depends on the kind of rose you desire.

Tubes Nos. 120 to 123 are for the rose bud, where the petals must be close together and turned in at the top.

Nos. 124 to 127 will produce a straighter petal for the regular rose.

Nos. 116 to 119 will make a curled or drooping petal for the rose in full bloom. The tube can be used for the last row of petals, and a straight rose tube such as No. 127 would be used for the inner rows of petals.

REVOLVING CAKE DECORATING STAND

Decorators will find a revolving cake decorating stand to be almost a "must." The decorating stand that you buy should revolve smoothly and be heavy enough to withstand tipping, as this would be a catastrophe in the middle of your decorating.

The Ateco revolving cake stand, as illustrated above, is made with all these features.

ROSES

The rose is considered the most important flower in the decorating field. It takes considerable practice to become proficient in making this flower, but the results are well worth the effort. The color range of this flower is wide and varied and its graceful petals add so much to the finished cake.

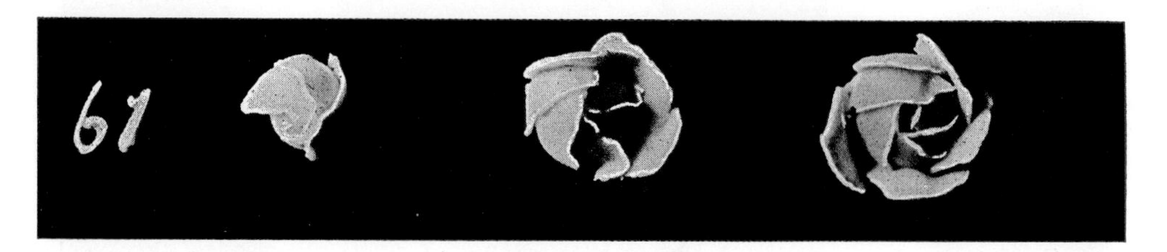

On the center of a No. 2 flower nail, with tube No. 61 and holding the bag in a vertical position, make four overlapping petals forming a bulb (which has a tiny opening at the top). Now around this bulb make five larger petals, holding the tube still in a vertical position, forming the center of the rose. Start the third row of petals, holding the tube in a somewhat horizontal position, allowing the petals to spread out.

The fourth and last row of petals is made by holding the tube in a bit more horizontal position, completing the outside large petals that enfold the rose. See Figs. 5–6–7 on page 57. The rose is never completed until pale green leaves have been added. This requires tube No. 66.

ROSE LEAVES

By holding the hand in a half way vertical position (using tube No. 66), press the icing out quickly and release with a twist of the wrist. It is customary to place from one to three leaves around the rose.

If larger roses are desired, use tubes Nos. 104, 124, 125, 126 or 127. Use leaf tubes Nos. 68, 69, 70 or 112 to make the proportionate leaves, and flower nail No. 7 should be substituted.

SWEET PEAS

These flowers are usually pale pink or white, and make a regal showing on the cake.

Sweet Peas can be made by holding tube No. 101 directly on the cake in a vertical position. Make a center petal by drawing tube upward in an arc towards you, using just a slight up and down wavy motion, tapering down nicely to a point.

Proceed with the second petal to the left of the first. Hold tube slanting to the left and proceed as you did with the first petal, only gradually turn slightly to the right so second petal tapers to the first petal.

For the third petal hold tube slanting to the right, gradually turn slightly to the left so that petal tapers nicely into center, completing flower.

In the lower part of illustration are two sweet peas on stems with leaves. Use a No. 4 tube and green icing for the stems, and No. 65 tube for the small leaves.

These illustrations are reproductions of cake tops decorated with plain and star tubes. Designs such as these are easy to make and are ideal suggestions for the beginner.

VIOLETS

In mixing colors for this luscious flower, use white butter cream as a base, and one drop of red with two drops of blue coloring. Continue this proportion until desired shade is reached. The correct shade of violet is an important factor, and must harmonize with other pastel colors on the cake.

On a No. 2 flower nail and holding tube No. 101 at an angle, make one petal to the left and one to the right, leaving room for the third petal which is placed on the top of the other petals and in the center. The third petal should overlap part of the first two petals. Take a No. 2 tube, with yellow butter cream, and make the yellow dots in the center of each blossom. Allow icing to dry on the nail prior to removing.

On the lower part of illustration is shown two flowers and a bud on stems. Use a No. 3 tube with green icing and make the stems first. Place flowers which have already been made, in position, and add a green seed pod to each.

To make the bud, use the violet icing with a No. 101 tube and make the bud right on the stem. Make three small curled-in petals close together in a sort of cup shape. Again using a No. 3 tube and green icing, fill in the base to resemble the lower part of the bud.

Larger violets are sometimes made with five petals, and in this case a No. 7 flower nail is used in conjunction with tube No. 61. Make the two larger petals on the top and the one large petal on the bottom. Tube No. 104 is used to make the little elongated petals on the side, and tube No. 2, with yellow butter cream, is used to make the yellow dots in the center of each blossom.

CARNATIONS

The Carnation, as you will note by the following illustration, is made with tube No. 102.

Make a cross on the cake slightly smaller than the size of the contemplated carnation, and draw an incomplete circle only covering three quarters of the cross. This acts as a guide in making flower petals (see illustration), the fourth quarter being left open for the seed pod, which is piped on last.

Take tube No. 102 and fill bag with white, pink or red icing. Make ruffled petals by holding the tube on an angle and move hand backward and forward. Make the length of the petals uneven by having some short and some long, making a ragged appearance of the carnation. Make about eight or ten of these petals in the three-quarter circle.

On top of this row add about eight more petals—these a little shorter than the shortest ones in the first row.

Hold tube upright and make about six more petals which stand up instead of lying flat for the top row.

After practicing, it will not take long for the appraising eye to judge the amount of petals to place on the flower. It will soon become second nature to make artistic and lifelike looking flowers. After completing flower, if you are looking for a ragged effect, snip each petal with scissors.

Now with No. 4 plain tube and pale green icing, make the seed pod with about six points at the top, as illustrated, then make three more drawn points at the bottom of pod to resemble sprouting leaves. Finish off with stem as shown, and complete by adding a few leaves. We suggest you use a No. 7 flower nail if the flowers are not being made directly on the cake.

White and pink carnations can be made more beautiful by tinting the edges of the petals with a brush, using a deeper pink icing.

Green carnations make an attractive decoration for the St. Patrick's Day cake, when used in conjunction with the proverbial green hat, the shamrock, harp or flag.

The illustration below is an excellent cake for the beginner. This daintily decorated Mother's Day cake gives you an idea of how the carnations can be arranged.

NARCISSUS

There are few flowers more beautiful, or interesting to make, than those depicting the Easter Season. These include narcissus, jonquils and daffodils, which are known as the trumpet flowers. You will note in the following illustration, given in a step by step method, that they are quite easy to make.

The narcissus is a six petal flower made with tube No. 103 on a No. 8 flower nail.

With white butter cream, press out six elongated petals completing a circle. Start each petal by holding the tube sideways on the outer rim of the flower nail, and make the petals narrow and sort of pinched in at the point, then turn tube slightly upwards, giving the petal a slight upward curl on the right side which not only improves the appearance but at the same time makes the necessary room for the next petal.

With tube No. 3 and bright yellow icing, place a stack of little circles on top of one another. Finish by dipping a small brush in bright orange coloring and make a fine line at the top of the circle.

Narcissus leaves, with tube No. 67, should be made in pale green, to which a bit of yellow has been added.

These illustrations are reproductions of cake tops decorated with plain and star tubes. Designs such as these are easy to make and are ideal suggestions for the beginner.

POPPIES

Poppies are made with tube No. 104, with colors running from burnt orange and salmon, to vivid scarlet red. We prefer the deep vivid red for this flower, bringing to our minds the poppies at Flanders Field.

Make the first petal flat on the cake with a slight wavy motion as illustrated.

Make a second petal on the left, third on the right, each overlapping about half of the first petal.

The fourth petal is made directly under the third, by holding the tube at an angle and making it stand nearly upright.

The final petal is made standing straight up, partly overlapping the fourth petal.

In center of flower, using tube No. 2, place a mound of black icing dots. With tube No. 4, and pale green icing, add the seed pod as shown in illustration. Add stems with darker icing and, with tube No. 102, make a scarlet bud as shown. A few green leaves will complete the flower, using tube No. 65.

SET No. 782

The decorator needs a good assortment of tubes for the basic decorations shown throughout this book. We recommend the set illustrated, in a permanent plastic box with transparent cover. This consists of a fairly complete assortment, including several special drop flower tubes.

PHANTASY FLOWERS
(Drop Flowers)

The little phantasy tubes come in many shapes and sizes; the flowers are quickly and easily made, giving great charm and that much-desired professional touch.

The tubes, with their respective decorations, shown on this page and pages 73, 74 and 75, are made with one press and a quick release of the bag. Use contrasting colors for the seed pods.

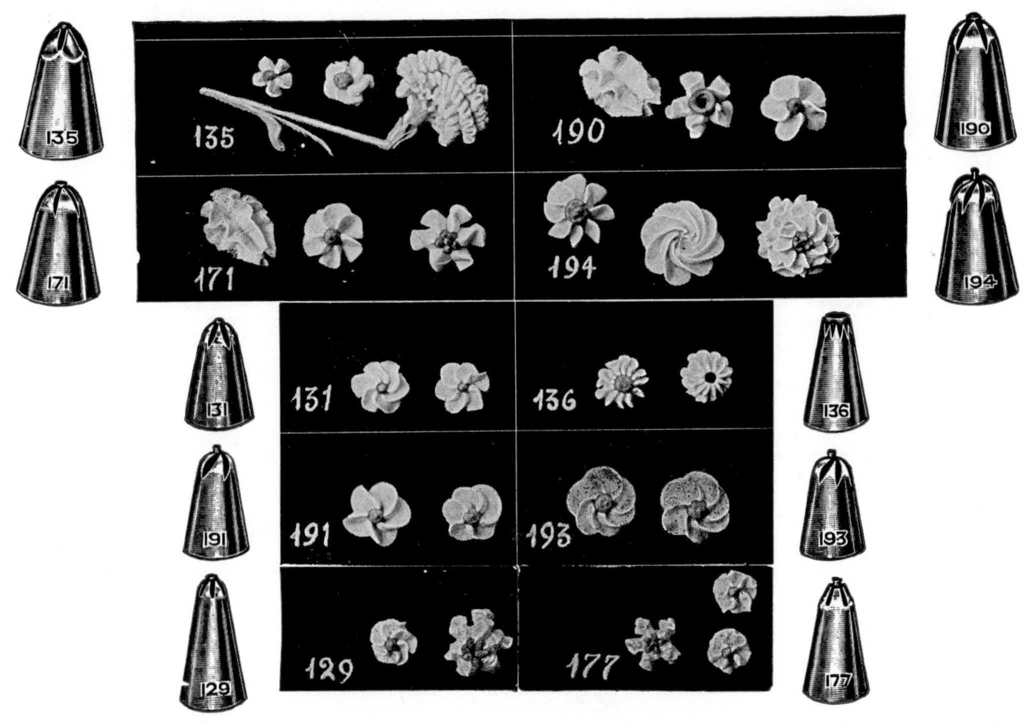

Many of these flowers are made by touching the cake with the tube until sufficient icing has emerged to form a flower. A slightly firmer icing than usual should be used. You will find these little push flowers complement the larger and more specific decorations.

Just a word of explanation regarding the illustrations of these special drop flower tubes and their decorations.

Tube No. 135 shows a good imitation of a carnation. This is made by holding the tube at a slight angle and using a slight wavy motion. Work across in an arc and back and forth, one row on top of another.

Tubes No. 171 and 190 show good decorations for French pastry, as well as the regular drop flowers.

What an idea for an engagement party!
Two separate heart cakes frosted together, covered with flowers.

Here are a few ideas for your Petit Fours,
but certainly do not be limited to these.

Here's a good idea for a formal wedding cake, with flowers cascading down the tiers.

We couldn't forget Dad on his day, and the real pipe certainly adds to the occasion.

Tube No. 194 is an exceptionally popular tube of this series. The illustration in the center is made by giving the tube one complete turn. This swirled flower does resemble a rose. The last flower of this illustration is an imitation of a dahlia. Just press and turn back and forth and gradually lift the tube while the icing is flowing.

Tube No. 136 is a popular daisy tube. It also serves as a candle holder when the center seed pod is not filled.

The phantasy flower is a boon to the decorator, as it not only may be used for beauty, but is a joy as a support, and for making repairs when a flaw has occurred.

Drop flower tubes for phantasy flowers have a wide range of versatility. Below we are illustrating another series of these drop flower tubes which are used to make the forget-me-not. Use a pale blue icing for the forget-me-not and fill in the center with a drop of yellow. Tubes Nos. 137 to 140 inclusive can be used for this flower in various degrees of size.

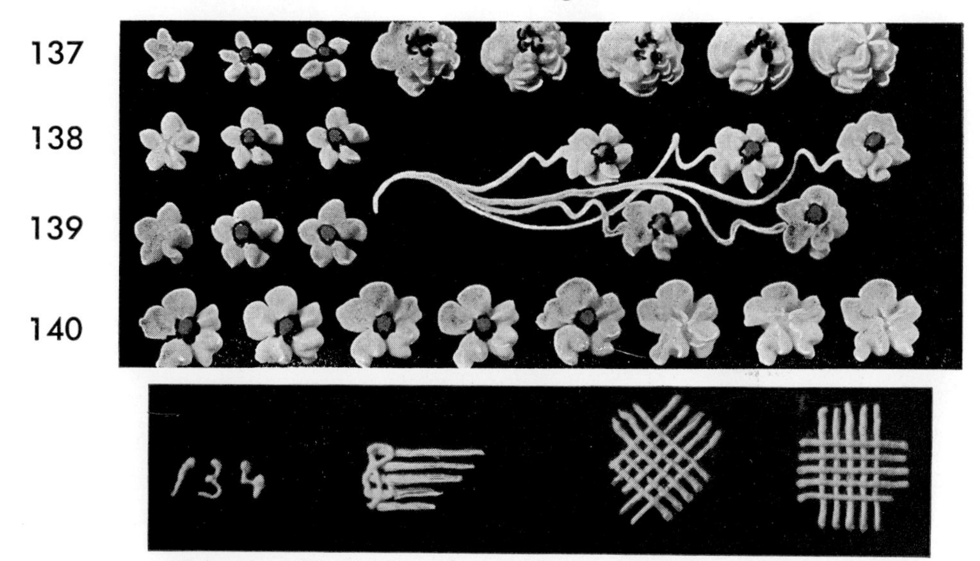

Tube No. 134—five line tube used for musical staffs and lattice work.

Tube No. 172—large fine star design—larger but the same design as No. 199.

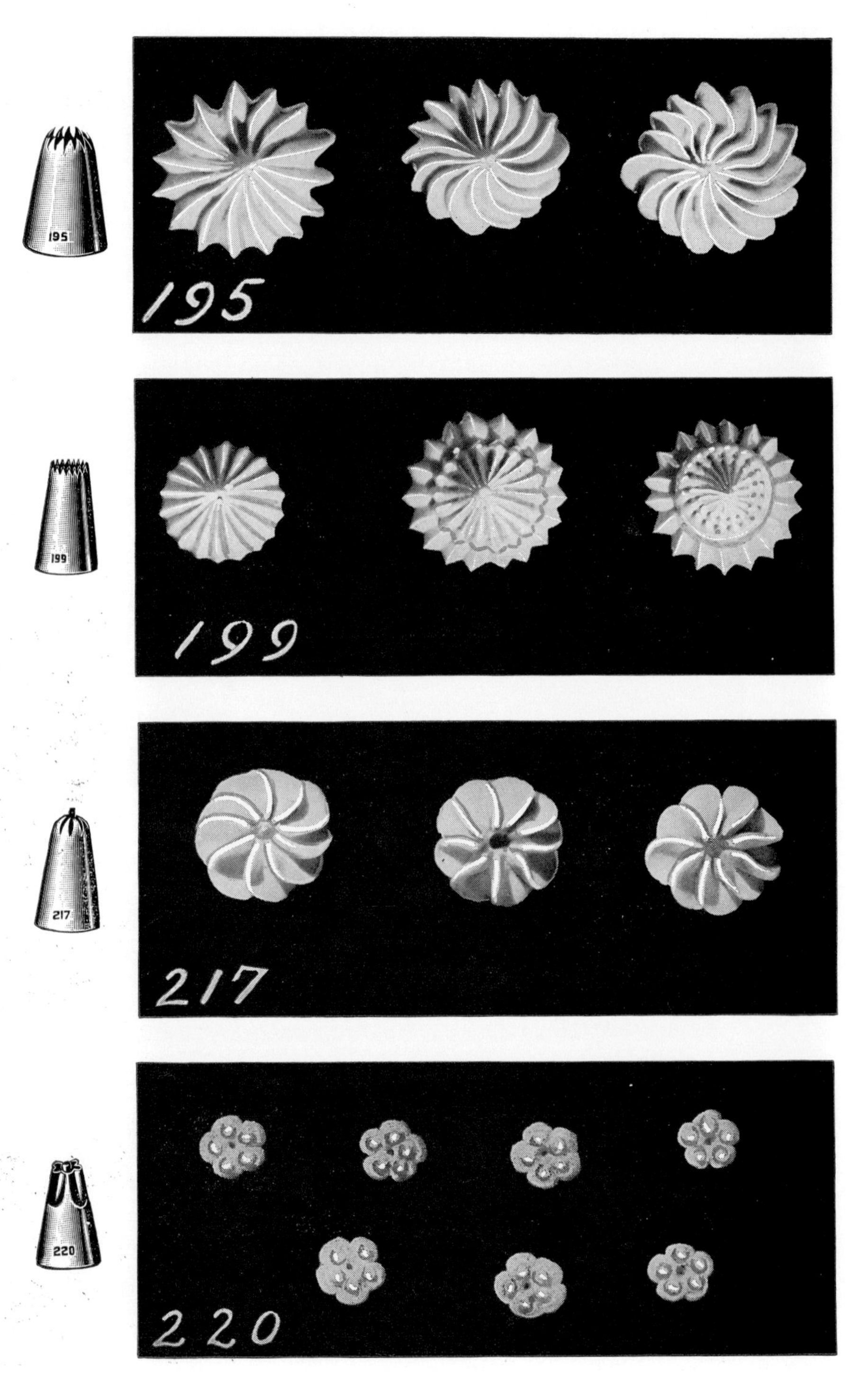
195
195
199
199
217
217
220
220

221

221
223
224
225

BASKET WORK

An excellent design for a cake is a basket with a bouquet of flowers. However, those who are interested in working with marzipan or almond paste will find a basket of fruit an attractive decoration for their cake.

Tubes Nos. 46 to 48° can be used for the serrations of baskets. It is a good idea to have the icing fairly stiff so that the serrations of these tubes stand out prominently. Plain tubes Nos. 2, 3 or 4 are usually used for the vertical staves. In the particular work shown on this and the following page, tube No. 47 was used for the wicker and tube No. 3 for the staves.

Make a general outline of your basket on the cake, including the handle.

Put in every other vertical stave within the border of the basket, using a plain tube (See Fig. A)

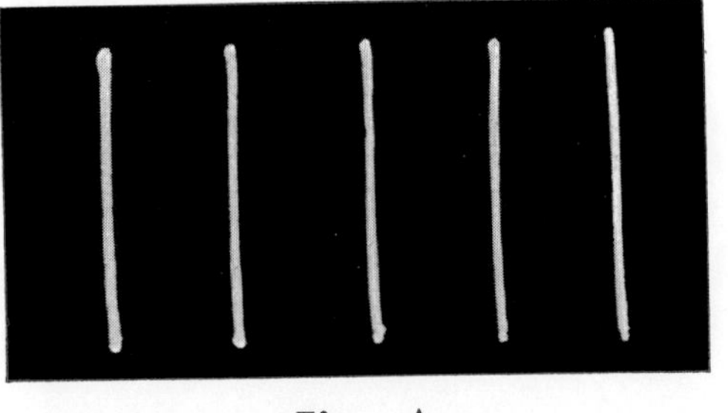

Fig. A

Change to the ribbon tube and decorate every other horizontal wicker. (See Fig. B)

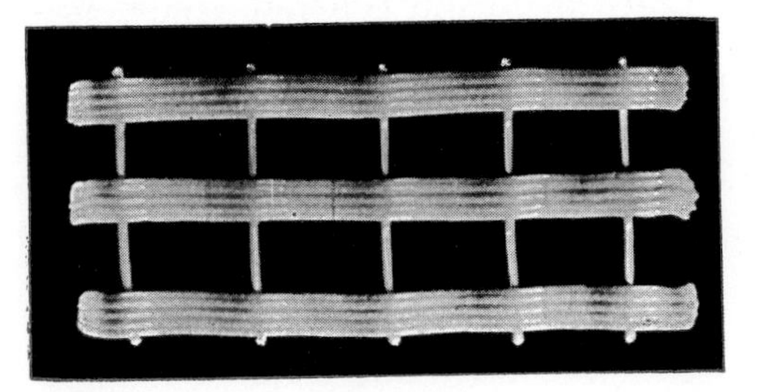

Fig. B

Again switching to the plain tube, put in the remaining vertical staves. (See Fig. C)

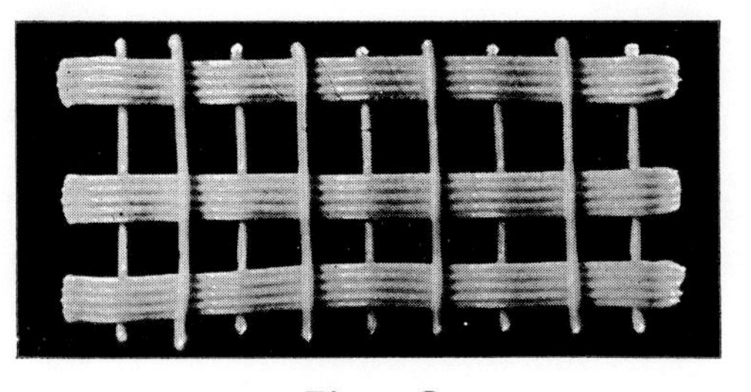

Fig. C

Now, finally switching back to the ribbon tube, decorate the remaining horizontal wickers. These are all short wickers only covering every other vertical stave (those put on in Fig. C). This will give the effect that the lattice work is woven over and under each other (See Fig. D)

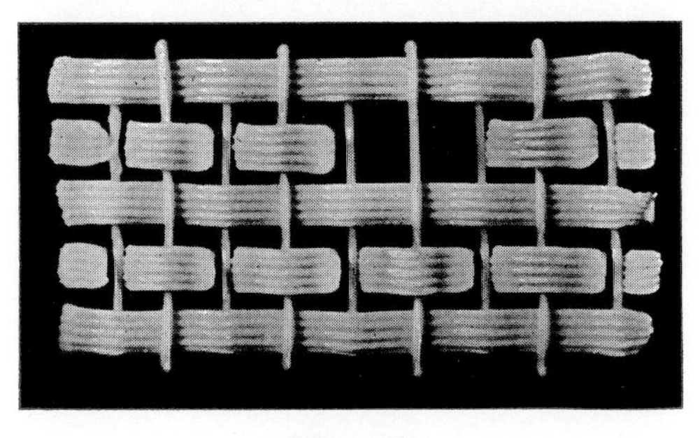

Fig. D

Finish your basket with an outside rim and handle, using a star tube such as No. 27 (see page 20 for the basket illustration using tube No. 27).

These illustrations have been made with space in between the lattice work to demonstrate more clearly the four steps. In the actual decoration, make the lattice work closer together, leaving no space between the wicker rows.

Use a darker icing for the staves and a lighter icing for the wicker. The contrasting colors help to make the work stand out more prominently.

APPLE CREAM PIE

COOKIES OR
JELLY MARGUERITES

Numbers indicate the tube used for each design

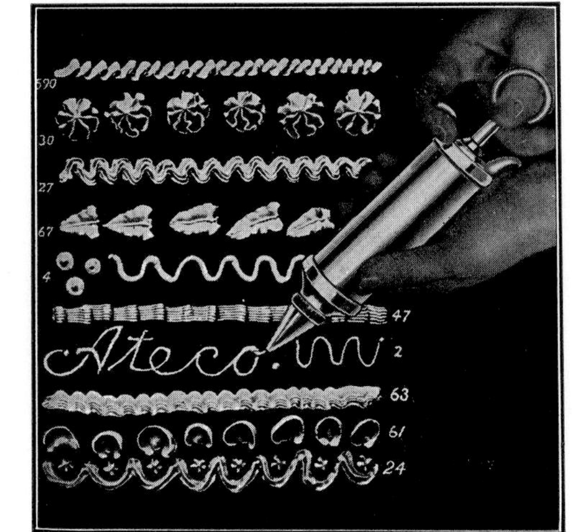

FRENCH PASTRY

ECLAIRS